PSYCHOANALYSIS AND HISTORY Special Issue

VOL. 11 NO. 2 2009

PSYCHOANALYSIS, FASCISM AND FUNDAMENTALISM

edited by Julia Borossa and Ivan Ward

Edinburgh University Press

© Edinburgh University Press Ltd, 2009

Published by Edinburgh University Press Ltd
22 George Square, Edinburgh EH8 9LF

Typeset in TimesTen
by SR Nova, India, and
Printed and bound by CPI Group (UK) Ltd, Croydon, CR0 4YY

A CIP record for this book is available from the British Library

ISBN 978 0 7486 3966 3 (paperback)

The right of the contributors
to be identified as authors of this work
has been asserted in accordance with
the Copyright, Designs and Patents Act 1988.

CONTENTS

Special Issue: Psychoanalysis, Fascism and Fundamentalism

FOREWORD

Julia Borossa and Ivan Ward, London, UK

The papers making up this Special Issue of *Psychoanalysis and History* are the record of a conference held in London on 29 and 30 November 2008, itself the result of a collaboration between the Centre for Psychoanalysis, Middlesex University, the Freud Museum, London and The Société Internationale d'Histoire de la Psychiatrie et de la Psychanalyse (SIHPP), Paris. The very first planning discussion took place almost two years ago between Elisabeth Roudinesco, president of the SIHPP and one of the guest editors, on a long walk through East London, taking in Brick Lane, an iconic London street which bears the history of successive waves of migrants into the capital, and whose present creative exuberance allows for the different idioms of and fruitful co-existence between its most recent incomers, the London Bangladeshi community, and urban youth culture. It was a fitting location for that first discussion which already touched on questions of hospitality, politics and creativity that would become central themes of the project.

It was decided that London would host the next annual conference (the XXIInd) of the SIHPP, that this conference would question and explore the potential of psychoanalysis to engage with the most current and pressing social and political issues, of which fundamentalism stood out with particular urgency, and that it would do so with an *a priori* openness, which would look broadly and without forceful agenda at many different forms of fundamentalist intolerance and hatred of the other. It was also clear to us that such a topic was intrinsically subject to historicization, and Fascism was introduced as a third organizing term, with respect to making a link back

JULIA BOROSSA is the Director of the Centre for Psychoanalysis at Middlesex University, the editor of *Sándor Ferenczi: Selected Writings* (Penguin, 1999) and the author of *Hysteria* (Icon Books, 2001) and of several essays on the history and social and political context of psychoanalytic thought. She is currently researching the question of the extensibility of psychoanalysis. Address for correspondence: Centre for Psychoanalysis, Middlesex University, Town Hall, The Burroughs, London NW4 4BT. [j.borossa@mdx.ac.uk]

IVAN WARD is Deputy Director of the Freud Museum and editor of the *Ideas in Psychoanalysis* series published by Icon Books. Address for correspondence: The Freud Museum, 20 Maresfield Gardens, London NW3 5SX. [ivan@freud.org.uk]

Psychoanalysis and History 11(2), 2009

to the discourses that helped shore up perverse notions of belonging in the first half of the 20th century.

In the course of subsequent discussions between the two guest editors, who took on the main organizing role, 'Psychoanalysis, Fascism and Fundamentalism' emerged as the title of the conference and of the resulting publication. As Jacqueline Rose points out in her paper, there is an inherent risk in aligning these terms, of putting them on a virtual equal footing and letting them simply co-exist for a while. We were very much aware that psychoanalysis is not a transparent discourse in itself and, for all its potential for unsettling, problematizing and opening up hardened debates, nothing exempts it from becoming either object, target or accomplice of motivations that may enter into the formation of the other two terms. We were taking two inter-related decisions: in addition to laying the three terms side by side, we wanted to provide a truly hospitable and interdisciplinary forum of exchange whereby a wide range of contributors would be invited to approach the topic from the perspective of the clinic, the academy and the arts. We were aware of the potential for ambiguity and even dissent and cacophony, not only in relation to the contribution of psychoanalysis, as indicated above, but also in as much as it is certainly possible, for example, for one reading to emphasize the similarities between Fascism and fundamentalism, and another to see them as being radically opposed.

As far as our aim for hospitality is concerned, this was seriously compromised when we realized that under the sway of a very recent tightening of the regulations governing how visas (now including the biometric data of applicants) are to be issued, and the devolution of responsibility for this task from the Foreign Office to the Home Office, the British Consulate in Cairo had failed to process Joseph Massad's travel documents in time to enable him to come. Glenn Bowman, who was to chair the session in question, kindly stepped in to read the paper, and we all worked hard to establish a telephone link between London and Cairo for the questions. This very inadequate, but rather moving solution sadly highlighted the politics of securitization and distrust under which we are increasingly forced to function.

In the shadow of the First World War, in the beautiful little essay 'On transience' Freud had written:

> [...] the war broke out and robbed the world of its beauties. It destroyed not only the beauty of the countrysides through which it passed and the works of art which it met with on its path but it also shattered our pride in the achievement of our civilization, our admiration for many philosophers and artists and our hopes of a final triumph over the differences between nations and races. It tarnished the lofty impartiality of our science, it revealed our instincts in all their nakedness and let loose the evil spirits within us which we thought had been tamed for ever by centuries of continuous education by the noblest minds. It made our country small again and made the rest of the world far remote. (Freud 1916[1915], p. 307)

So we have necessarily lost our innocence, but we must not for all that give in to cynicism and the paranoia of a divisive securitization which will never make us – in *this* small country – feel safe enough.

Psychoanalysis does not have the answers to the problems of our times, of course. Its strength is precisely in its capacity to resist the temptation of being the master discourse. It can and has been the accomplice as well as the target of politically repressive regimes, but it has also resisted them in quite unexpected ways, as Daniel Pick's paper shows. Nevertheless, it has shown itself guilty more often than not of a lack of hospitality to the culturally other, as Joseph Massad argues here. It has at times conspired to make 'the rest of the world' feel very far away indeed.

But its strength, and we do wish to stress this in our Foreword, lies in teaching us to tolerate ambivalence and uncertainty, to allow questions to be posed and responsibility to be taken by each subject for the motivations of his or her desire. We did take a risk in choosing not to inflect how the contributors and the audience would respond to the conjuncture of the three terms. As Clare Winnicott once stated about the phenomenology of her practice:

> Of course we shall not always understand what is going on or what they are trying to convey to us and often this does not matter. What matters most is that we respond in a way that conveys our *willingness to try to understand* [...] This in itself can provide a therapeutic experience. (Winnicott 1963, p. 173)

The cover image, a photograph taken by David Modell of a balaclava-clad animal rights activist cradling a kitten, speaks of this ambivalence. Enigmatic and awkward, it juxtaposes tenderness and violence. The masked figure is threatening, yet the vulnerability and fear in his eyes invite more complex identifications. And, indeed, the accompanying essays, as did the conference presentations on which they are based, will inevitably raise more questions than they will answer and will not be offering the comfort of a unified point of view.

Both the conference and this volume open with Daniel Pick's account of the historical encounter between psychoanalysis and Fascism, exemplified in the pathography of Rudolph Hess and in post-war theorizations of group psychology with their increasing emphasis on the concept of the superego. In very different ways, Caroline Rooney and Fakhry Davids take up themes of disappointment, humiliation and exclusion. The former uses literary examples to discuss how a fundamentalist or Fascist 'psychic structure' may come to be, seeing this configuration as part of a life history that is not to do with a rejection of modernity (as is often claimed) but rather a rejection *by* modernity. The latter examines the complex motivations of a young Muslim man, his radicalization within the context of post-9/11 Islamophobia and 'everyday racism', and the paranoia resulting from his attempt to reconcile conflicting loyalties and identifications. Fundamentalist ideology in this case (and in many others) performed a containing function for adolescent turmoil, a form of restitution for earlier disappointments, a vehicle to transfer blame and guilt, and a legitimated way to express oedipal rage.

Using a different medium, fundamentalist ideology was explored in some of the documentary films shown and discussed by David Modell. It was the sense of conviction and fixity of belief that most interested him, drawing surprising connections between people committed to Christian fundamentalism, far right politics and animal rights activism. The subjects of his films were drawn to their beliefs through complex histories that revealed hidden stories of narcissistic injury. Adherence to the ideal and membership of the group provided the stabilizing factor in their lives. Rooney's idea of 'chronic disappointment' is an attempt to embrace the social and psychological dimensions of political motivation in a suggestive term. It is always *complex*, and Mohsin Hamid, reading from and discussing his novel *The Reluctant Fundamentalist*, evoked the subtle transformative effects of the 'vicissitudes of life' and how they interact with the mythopoeia of the internal world. Somewhere at the heart of fundamentalism, according to Hamid, is the narrative of a 'romantic quest'.

The question of values is fundamental to psychoanalysis, yet largely unspoken. Identifying psychoanalysis as a post-Enlightenment 'liberal' discourse (an ascription that receives widespread assent), Joseph Massad argues that the identification with liberalism exemplified in the work of North African analysts living in the West results in a misapprehension of Islam that denies its intellectual history and plurality. In another close reading of a text, Stephen Frosh starts with a discussion of a closed fundamentalist position in Jewish biblical exegesis, and, taking his cue from Emanuel Levinas, reads it against the grain to allow for the possibility of ambivalence. Certainties and fixed beliefs – in this case about Jewish entitlement in Palestine – are undermined and destabilized through a 'psychoanalytic' reading.

Finally, it was in an uncertain world of Jewish, Catholic and 'Greek' identifications – and the universal aspirations of psychoanalysis within this triad – that Elisabeth Roudinesco found her intellectual path and her conviction that 'a certain kind of materialism' can include an intimation of the 'divine' within the human. Her personal and moving account was responded to with equal grace and thought by Jacqueline Rose, who questioned the deeply felt assumption – the *wish* as she called it – that psychoanalysis itself can ward off the 'two historical monstrosities' of Fascism and fundamentalism. That may be an illusion yet perhaps Freud's discovery is still a source of hope, where 'we should continue to look for a way of thought that most radically challenges systems of belief that today seem once again to have the power to place the whole world in peril' (Rose, p. 268).

What unfortunately is not included in the issue is the breadth of the audience response to the papers, where what strongly emerged were various disappointments in the failures of socialism and, as Roudinesco, Rooney and Rose all address, the need for some kind of faith that is not authoritarian, which can be expressed as just the need to maintain faith with each other. We hope that readers of this issue will treat this as a work in progress in developing their own responses to the material.

The guest editors are grateful to John Forrester, editor of *Psychoanalysis and History*, for providing such a fitting home for our project.

References

Freud, S. (1916[1915]) On transience. *Standard Edition* 14, pp. 304–7. London: Hogarth.

Winnicott, C. (1963) Face to face with children. In: J. Kanter (ed.), *Face to Face with Children: The Life and Work of Clare Winnicott*, pp. 166–83. London: Karnac, 2004.

DOI: 10.3366/E1460823509000361

Articles

'IN PURSUIT OF THE NAZI MIND?'
THE DEPLOYMENT OF PSYCHOANALYSIS IN THE
ALLIED STRUGGLE AGAINST GERMANY

Daniel Pick, London, UK

I

This paper focuses on the history of the encounter between psychoanalysis and Fascism, and especially on investigations of the Nazi leadership during the Second World War.[1] It serves here to provide one significant historical context for the other contributions to the special issue, which focus more specifically upon contemporary problems. Its final section offers an example of wartime discussion, drawn from observations of Rudolf Hess, deputy Führer of the Nazi Party. Hess fell into the hands of the British authorities in 1941. He was soon perceived to be mentally ill and his treatment was written up by his doctors (Rees *et al.* 1947). They sought to make sense of his private, even unconscious, system of beliefs, and to analyse the subliminal attractions of Hitler. This was an inquiry based, to some degree, on clinical contact rather than, as in a number of other studies (not least those of Hitler himself), distant speculations upon a Nazi's 'internal world'.

There are various ways to date Fascism, but I have in mind here the period from 1919 to 1946 – that is, from the rise of the organized movement in Italy to the conclusion of the main Nuremberg Trial. The 1920s and 1930s also

---

1. This account was presented in abbreviated form at the Conference on Psychoanalysis, Fascism and Fundamentalism organized by the Freud Museum in November 2008. Full references to sources referred to here will be given in my forthcoming book *In Pursuit of the Nazi Mind* (Oxford University Press).

DANIEL PICK is professor of history at Birkbeck, University of London. He is an editor of *History Workshop Journal* and an associate member of the British Psychoanalytical Society. His publications include: *Faces of Degeneration. A European Disorder, c.1848–c.1918* (Cambridge University Press, 1989); *War Machine: The Rationalisation of Slaughter in the Modern Age* (Yale University Press, 1993); *Svengali's Web: The Alien Enchanter in Modern Culture* (Yale University Press, 2000); and *Rome or Death: The Obsessions of General Garibaldi* (Cape, 2005). He is the co-editor (with Lyndal Roper) of *Dreams and History: The Interpretation of Dreams from Ancient Greece to Modern Psychoanalysis* (Routledge, 2004). Address for correspondence: School of History, Classics and Archaeology, Birkbeck, University of London, Malet Street, London WC1E 7HX. [d.pick@bbk.ac.uk]

Psychoanalysis and History 11(2), 2009

of course marked the last period of Freud's work as well as the first of Melanie Klein's. How did psychoanalysis contribute to or reflect modern understanding of the catastrophe of interwar politics? How did it seek to combat the dire developments in Germany? The answer, judging by a *Guardian* review of George Makari's history of psychoanalysis, *Revolution in Mind* (Makari 2008), appears to be not at all:

> But this is what finally seems so troubling in the history of psychoanalysis. Bound up with the confining of significance to an interior world, with a dismissal of facts and insouciance as to what really happened, is a fatal neglect of reality. Members of the psychoanalytic confraternity who suggested utilising Freud's theories in the political realm ... were shouted down. We get every possible permutation of theory, interminable shifts of emphasis and twiddling with minutiae. Yet during the squabbles and quibbles, Germany was suppurating. Missing the real crisis, these doctors and intellectuals (most of them Jewish) were fiddling with themselves and their silly theories while Rome was beginning to burn. (O'Grady 2008, p. 7)

This characterization is certainly a gross over-simplification, indeed in many respects a travesty. The present paper suggests some of the diverse ways that psychoanalysis was actively deployed in an attempt to combat the Nazi threat and argues that a more nuanced history of the relationship is required. That would entail reading more closely what was actually produced, and thereby to rescue what were in fact strikingly different psychoanalytical endeavours from later caricatured accounts. Some analysts, no doubt, were slow to see the extent of the danger, politically myopic, or worse, but psychoanalysis also pitched itself in a variety of ways directly against Fascism. The book burnings conducted at the beginning of the Third Reich exemplified Nazi antipathy towards psychoanalysis, and indeed towards any meaningful psychotherapeutic ethos. Freud's work was of course in very good company on the fires in Berlin. To emphasize Nazi hatred for psychoanalysis is not to deny the discomforting history of 'fellow travelling', by some practitioners, nor to disregard the development of the notorious Göring Institute in Berlin, nor still Freud's slowness to break off relations during the 1930s with those who continued to practise in Germany under the Nazis.[2]

The relationship of Jung and his early followers to developments in the Third Reich is another complex story that has been considered in various recent studies, notably by Andrew Samuels (1992a, 1992b) and Sonu

---

2. The perversion of psychoanalysis in the Third Reich led to considerable trouble after 1945 when the IPA had to decide what to do with the dubious remnants of a once thriving Society. This is well covered in a number of recent studies, notably Cocks (1985). The dilemma is fascinatingly illustrated in the British psychoanalyst, John Rickman's reports for the IPA and the British Society, published in a valuable collection by Pearl King (2003). Martin Dehli (2009) also throws light on this vexed post-war history.

Shamdasani (2003). Jung's followers divided on this issue during the 1930s, but his own political equivocations, amounting to tacit support for Nazism at one stage, were to be modified and even reversed later on. Nonetheless, a number of statements by him, not least his account of 'Jewish psychology' in 'The state of psychotherapy today' (Jung 1934), reveal plainly enough the toxic anti-Semitic strain in his thought. Needless to say, recognition of Jung's uncomfortable, even sinister, political accommodation at that time is not to discount other aspects of his thought and influence, nor to ignore important shifts in his position.

Several historical inquiries have sought to use psychoanalysis (or sometimes even psychiatry) to understand the origins or consequences of the German political crisis. But the majority of recent major historical works on Fascism and Nazism (I won't review the distinction between those two terms carefully here, although I am in the main talking of the German development) have viewed Freudian approaches as marginal, or even antithetical, to proper historical inquiry. The reasons for this view would merit more scrutiny than I can provide in this brief introduction, but suffice to say that, particularly after its emergence in the USA in the 1950s, 'psychohistory' acquired a bad reputation for sweeping generalizations, 'wild analysis' and reductionism.

In noting the undoubted sins of commission or omission in some of that literature (and indeed in some of Freud's own controversial historical forays), there is a risk that we may neglect the fact that psychological theories of one kind or another suffused the 'primary' literature surrounding Fascism, not just a later, 'secondary' literature. Whether or not we now approve of applied psychoanalysis in history, anti-Fascist commentaries in the interwar and immediate post-war period were significantly shaped by ideas about what people are like, derived from psychoanalysis, and are thus part of the cultural and intellectual history at stake. Moreover, when historians hark back to the Freudian investigations of Nazism, there has been a tendency to conflate very different approaches.

II

Recall the quotation: 'Missing the real crisis, these doctors and intellectuals (most of them Jewish) were fiddling with themselves and their silly theories while Rome was beginning to burn' (O'Grady 2008, p. 7). In defence of this one might, conceivably, point to psychoanalytic work that remained focused remorselessly upon abstract theoretical concerns, or exclusively with the internal politics of the institution itself. But the charge here seems deeper and broader – that psychoanalysis had nothing much to say or contribute to the struggle against Nazism, indeed that it was narcissistically self-absorbed and failed to attend to the massive crisis unfolding in Europe.

Let us leave aside the dubious rhetorical purpose of the parenthesis within that quotation and the jibe about the quality of the work ('silly theories'). In response to the main criticism ('missing the real crisis'), one might need first to give some thought to those practitioners who did take up Freud's or Klein's concepts, or those of other key psychoanalytical thinkers, in interpreting group psychology in general or Fascist mass politics in particular, during the period of the movement's inception and catastrophic development. The resulting psychoanalytic work, as mentioned, was varied in format and in theoretical orientation. There were publications on war, militarism, ultra-nationalism and reports for government agencies, international bodies, the army or intelligence services. Others developed innovative new screening and interviewing techniques. The war witnessed a number of experimental approaches to the treatment of what was known as 'war neurosis' – that is, the psychiatric casualties of the conflict, and here again psychoanalytic thought played an important part.

Any inventory of this type would need to include the work of Reich, Anna Freud, Menninger, Bion, Glover, Rickman, Jones, Money-Kyrle, Fromm, Bowlby, Erikson, Simmel, Langer, Bettelheim, Jacobson, Alexander, Kris. The list could easily be much enlarged but even that assortment of names is enough to suggest the scale of interventions, of one kind or another, made directly in response to the crisis. We might debate the quality of each of these contributions, but suffice to say that there was a shared endeavour to understand both the psycho-social conditions in which the extreme right flourished and the unconscious factors that made Fascism attractive to so many. Close reading of clinical material itself in and around the war, including notably Melanie Klein's, reveals how heavily it was shadowed by the horrors taking place in the outside world. This is richly illustrated in some of her published case material as well as in the references to Hitler, to bombing, to war, in case notes contained in the unpublished Klein archives now housed at the Wellcome Trust. There were also a variety of concepts – think, for instance, of Anna Freud's (1937) 'identification with the aggressor' – that quickly came to seem relevant to the study of Fascism even if not directly prompted by it. Psychoanalysis had much to say about the seductions of Fascist ideology as well as (perhaps from our point of view more tendentiously) the psychopathology of individual Nazi leaders.

By the interwar period, there were several different Freudian accounts of the mind. Some interpreters (such as the aforementioned, increasingly dissident and troubled figure of Reich) had drawn on Marx as well as early Freud – for example, *The Three Essays*, '"Civilized" sexual morality and modern nervous illness'; others relied most substantially upon work that had been published in the first phase of organized Fascism itself: notably *Beyond The Pleasure Principle*, *Group Psychology and the Analysis of the Ego*, *The Ego and the Id* (crucially the paper where Freud most fully presented the concept of the 'superego'). *The Ego and the Id* was in fact published in the year after Mussolini's March on Rome, and in the same year as Hitler's failed putsch in Munich which had led to his imprisonment for the best part of the following year, 1924. In prison, Hitler wrote (with assistance from Hess and others) *Mein Kampf,* his own tendentious *Bildungsroman,* a story of supposed psychological 'awakening' and true revelation. Freud's post-1918 works had their clinical and theoretical rationale but, as has often been remarked, they also had an immediate political purchase on contemporary mass politics and the demagogic role of Fascist leaders. This anticipation of the spiral into Fascism in Freud's 'Group Psychology' paper is brilliantly described in a later important contribution to the psycho-political literature, Adorno's 'Freudian theory and the pattern of Fascist propaganda' (Adorno 1951).

Still keeping in mind the reviewer's claim above, note the dire personal circumstances and consequences of the Third Reich for Freud's followers as well as for the Freud family. The situation after the *Anschluss* – Anna's meeting with the Gestapo, the final, very late departure from Vienna to Paris and London, the murder of Freud's sisters in the camps, which occurred after his own death in London – are covered in several important extant studies. Many of the most influential analysts who developed Freud's ideas, on both sides of the Atlantic after 1945, had been directly affected by Hitler's rise to power: whether, for instance, as refugees from Europe, therapists of Holocaust victims, army officers and/or contributors to wartime intelligence. A number of psychoanalysts contributed to denazification projects in post-war Germany as well as to international organizations seeking to entrench democracy after the fall of the Third Reich. To continue biographically for a moment longer, we should not forget that some psychoanalysts endured direct persecution, in some cases death, under the Nazis, amongst whom Karl Landauer, founder of the Frankfurt Institute of Psychoanalysis who died at Bergen–Belsen. Numerous others were uprooted and forced to flee. These processes of upheaval and persecution were registered in many ways in the post-war literature.

Less well considered to date have been the various adaptations of psychoanalysis to a wider 'political science' of national cultural formations in the 1930s and beyond. We could usefully compare psychoanalytic endeavours here with visions of Fascism and militarism provided by cultural anthropologists, for instance, Margaret Mead, Ruth Benedict and Geoffrey Gorer. It would also be instructive to compare Freudian writings on the German question with the analysis of the Third Reich and the proposals for denazification made by sociologists such as Talcott Parsons. There are clearly links: Parsons, for instance, made significant use of the idea of the superego (Gerhardt 1993). The views of psychoanalysts were frequently canvassed by official agencies (surely far more than today) and clinicians thus rubbed shoulders with anthropologists, sociologists, economists and political scientists in thinking about how to avoid German *revanchism* at a number of wartime and post-war conferences, or within inter-disciplinary research projects for international organizations, such as UNESCO. The latter organized a long-running study of the tensions that militated against international understanding and amongst its contributors were Henry Dicks, Anna Freud and Erich Fromm. As 'denazification' projects gave way to a new 'Cold War' rhetoric in the late 1940s and the 1950s, some of these psycho-cultural inquiries continued in a new guise: totalitarianism rather than Fascism at the core of the investigation.

Another area where psychoanalytical thought, broadly defined, was politically engaged can be gleaned from the observational studies of the Nazis conducted at the Nuremberg trials, in prisoner of war camps and later in the German prison system (Dicks 1972). The clinical depictions produced at the end of the war had on many occasions afforded the first detailed 'characterological' accounts of the defeated leadership, a kind of 'oral history' of what Churchill had once called 'the Hitler gang', a plethora of psychological portraits written at close quarters. In some cases these were the only accounts that we have, as the subjects committed suicide or were executed. These were not necessarily directly psychoanalytic works, but the memoirs of Gilbert (1948), Goldensohn (2004) and others certainly reveal intriguing connections to Freudian thought and practice. If some of the medical and psychological assessments were structured or disguised 'interrogations', on other occasions the invitation and purpose were more free-floating, with the interviewer endeavouring to remain in a kind of 'abstinent' role whilst inviting the interviewees to say whatever came into their heads, without selection.

Alongside the work on perpetrators as well as psychoanalytic papers focusing upon their descendants (or, in the case of Mitscherlich and Mitscherlich [1975], the putative inability of a whole society to mourn), there are also of course many important reflections upon first, second, even third generation members of families who were persecuted by the Nazis. Of course there is a crucial distinction: to become a 'perpetrator' is to move from the idea or the fantasy to the act, and this places the subject, irrevocably, in a different position to that of the victim. Yet psychoanalysis has demonstrated again and again the psychic complexity of the place of 'Nazi' or 'Jew', the mobility of a 'Fascist state of mind' and of the defences against recognizing them; in short the many possible unconscious identifications and interactions that may occur in the face of unbearable suffering, guilt or responsibility.

III

The psychology of Fascism produced in the 1940s was not of course necessarily written through a Freudian lens, as we will see shortly in the case of Hess. Before the Nuremberg trials were under way, some consideration was given to a request that the defendants be shot in the chest rather than in the head in order for subsequent brain autopsies to be undertaken. In the end of course the chosen method of execution was hanging, as the firing squad, it was thought, might be seen as a more honourable mode of killing. But the request to conduct an inquiry into the brain is telling: as though the answer to Nazism might yet lie in some organic lesion or abnormality. One might link this request to the continuing cultural fascination with the fate of Hitler's skull and bones (enduring rumours that the remains were gathered up in Berlin and later analysed in a Moscow laboratory) to say nothing of the sustained psychiatric and wider cultural interest in the significance of physiognomy and heredity. Psychoanalysis, in other words, ran up against, or sometimes became blurred with other, more positivistic or biologistic approaches, or a kind of popular folklore about the Nazis.

To complement works such as Rosenbaum's (1998) *Explaining Hitler* (which tracks diverse portraits produced in historiography and high culture) or Kershaw's (1987) *The Hitler Myth* (which maps the myriad theories, fantasies and folklore surrounding the leader in and beyond his lifetime), it would be interesting to consider further the range of Nazi 'types' that emerged in wartime and post-war popular representations. Cinematic depictions from the 1940s, for instance, of hidden Nazi infiltrators might be compared and contrasted with psychoanalytic accounts of repressed 'Fascistic' propensities. Consider, for instance, Orson Welles's memorable characterization of an unrepentant Nazi lodged in an American village in *The Stranger* (1946). Edward G. Robinson, who, in this film, plays an investigator from the Allied Control Commission, retorts at one point that it would take a psychiatrist to understand the German catastrophe. Hitchcock's film *Lifeboat* (1944) examines a kind of Nazi psychopathy but then troubles its viewers' identification, or at least comfortable moral position, by showing the vicious and murderous feelings latent, and then explicit, in some of the Americans cast adrift on the sea with the German villain. Think also here of the secret Nazi cells depicted in two other Hitchcock films, *Saboteur* (1942) and *Notorious* (1946). In the latter, at least, the most ruthless feelings are by no means confined exclusively to the obvious, demarcated villains.

Much still remains to be investigated about the intellectual and cultural ramifications of wartime psychoanalytic work. How, I wonder, were the various forms of psychoanalytically-influenced profilings of Hitler and other Nazis (for instance, those that had been commissioned by the Office of Strategic Services during World War II) related to the later, much more extensive forms of profiling of foreign leaders undertaken routinely by organizations such as the CIA? How were the famous pioneering 'group therapy' approaches of Rickman and Bion, amongst others, in the treatment of British soldiers, related to the near contemporaneous 'screening' studies designed to expose the unconscious attitudes of those Germans seeking

rehabilitation and employment after 1945? There are indications that
the analytic attitude of Bion in relation to the group in the 'Northfield
experiments' was also carried over into the approaches of some analysts
working for the Allies after the war. There are interesting comments by
Roger Money-Kyrle and Henry Dicks, amongst others, about this, albeit
short-lived, applied psychoanalytic work for the Allied Control Commission
in occupied Germany. This style of project, which reprised the question
of the subject's slavish capitulation to a 'sadistic superego', foreshadowed
the landmark study of *The Authoritarian Personality* by Adorno *et al.*
(1950). The latter combined a substantial empirical dimension (surveys,
questionnaires, interviews) with political and psychoanalytic theories.
Famously, it provided an elaborate 'scale' of Fascist propensities.

The ideas of these wartime clinicians on denazification and the psycho-
social dynamics of 'blind obedience' keyed in with Bion's developing ideas
about 'basic assumption groups' and 'work groups', or, to put it another
way, with Klein's conceptualizations of the paranoid–schizoid position and
the depressive position. They also foreshadowed the famous experiments
of the Yale University psychologist, Stanley Milgram, originally performed
in 1963, published in 1964 and then in book form in 1974 in *Obedience
to Authority* (Fermlaglich 2006). Strikingly the American doctor and
psychoanalyst with a senior position in the US denazification/screening
programme in occupied Germany, David Levy, had sought to meet Dicks
(of whom more in a moment) and Bion as he passed through London on
his way to Germany just after the end of the war.[3]

IV

Before finally turning to Hess and his doctors, I want to recall an earlier
representation to be found in Riefenstahl's notorious film, *The Triumph
of the Will* [*Triumph des Willens,* 1935]. Hess was shown as he introduced
Hitler at the 1934 Nuremberg party meeting. He was demonstrably the
'warm up man' and served in this sequence of the film to embody the role
of the adoring underling. I excerpt below the relevant section of the film
script, bearing in mind that the images too, obviously unavailable here,
unlike at the conference at which this paper was first given, are central
to the overall effect. In this particular scene a close angle shot shows
Hess in uniform, approaching the speaker's podium in a large, packed hall.
There is an expectant atmosphere, the vast audience pictured awaiting this

3. Levy's fascinating papers, in which requests for these meetings are contained, are
available at the Oskar Diethelm Library at Cornell's Medical College in New York. For
Levy's correspondence on denazification, see boxes 34 and 35. On his planned London
visit, see, for instance, his letter dated 5 September 1945.

keynote opening address. Hess begins with a homage to the dead war leader, Hindenburg. As he reveres him, the film cuts to the audience, as well as to shots of approving foreign dignitaries ('esteemed representatives' from Imperial Japan, Fascist Italy and Fascist Spain). The editing juxtaposes Hess with images of German men, women, a child, showing us their close and attentive focus, as though the work of representation here was both to describe and to elicit in the cinema-viewer a kind of rapture.

Hess begins: 'I am opening this, our Sixth Party Congress, in respectful remembrance of Field Marshal, and President of the Reich... Von Hindenburg, who has passed into eternity. We remember the Field Marshal as the first soldier of the Great War, and, thus, also remember our fallen comrades.' Shots of Hess are interspersed with standards and banners of the Nazi Party, and with the image of a soldier, bearing the swastika. It is worth setting out the scripted dialogue as Hess paves the way for Hitler's own, climactic speech:

Shots of Hitler, seated.

Shot of audience surrounding Hitler.

Shot back at Hess:

HESS

... My Führer, ...

Shot back at Hitler seated.

Shots of Nazi banners, flags and NSDAP standards held by SA men in Audience.

HESS

(off camera)

... around you are gathered the flags and standards of National Socialism....

Back at Hess again, at podium: closer angle, though.

HESS

... Only when their cloth ...

NSDAP Party standards, flags and banners again.

HESS

(off camera)

... will have decayed, will humanity looking back, be able to comprehend what you, ...

Shot at Hitler's profile again.

HESS

(off camera)

... my Führer, mean to Germany. ...

(applause)

LONG SHOT: audience in massed hall, then:

Hess back at podium, smiling at enthusiasm of audience.

Hitler seated near podium again.

HESS

(off camera)

... You are Germany, when you act, the nation acts, when you judge, the people judge! ...

(applause, O.C.)

Hitler's expression is one of the utmost appreciation; then:

Back at Hess:

HESS

... Our gratitude is the pledge to stand by you, through good days and bad...

Shots of Göring, Bormann, etc.

HESS

(off camera)

... come whatever may!...

(applause on audio)

View of massed attendance in hall; then:

Back to Hess at podium.

HESS

... Thanks to your leadership, Germany will achieve her aim to become the homeland –...

(applause)

An elderly woman is seen expressing her approval to Hess's remarks during the speech; then:

HESS

(off camera)

... the homeland for all Germans in the world....

(applause)

Hitler pictured seated near podium again.

HESS

(off camera)

... You have been the guarantor of victory...

Back at Hess again:

HESS

... you are for us the guarantor of peace! Adolf Hitler!

Nazi cheers of 'heil' over soundtrack as...

... Hitler congratulates Hess by shaking his hand; Julius Streicher, Gauleiter of Upper Franconia stands in background smiling. [4]

Here the scene dissolves out. This piece of cinema raises a host of questions in its own right – how it works as propaganda, fostering the fervour, despite all Riefenstahl's later protestations to be simply making a documentary. The film presents us with Hess's own enactment of and commentary upon the need for obedience and idealization. This depiction has many resonances for a psychoanalytic account of Fascism. We may want to consider here in Hess's speech the imagined community and the implied 'other' at stake, as well as the cult of the dead that shadows his performance. What are we to make of the latent erotized tie, or again the curious evocation of the rotting cloth – it refers evidently to Nazi ritual, to the flags and so forth that are cut into the scene, but also unwittingly perhaps to the possibility of a day when this parade of purity will itself be reduced to putrefaction? Hess had risen with Hitler; he lived dutifully, perhaps more dutifully than any other, in his shadow. But I refer to this film material now by way of introducing the Hess who, a few years later, mysteriously took flight for Britain.

When Hess unexpectedly parachuted from his plane, to land near Glasgow in 1941, consciously intent upon a one-man peace-mission, he became both a prisoner and patient. He was cast as patient because of his manifest peculiarities and numerous 'complaints', physical and

---

4. Material taken from script available from: http://www.geocities.com/emruf4/triumph.html/

emotional, as well as the requirement to observe him very closely, following his apparent, attempted suicide not long after his captivity began. The conclusion was reached in short that he was in a state of mental disorder, although how far this constituted a serious psychiatric condition was much debated. Either way he was deemed suitable for close medico-psychiatric observation. As noted earlier, the Hess case is particularly interesting as, unlike so many more speculative reports of the time, there was a 'here and now' aspect to the work.

Hess came to Britain with a complex back-story. Speculation about his mental state had existed in Nazi circles before the war–some rumours had circulated about his sexuality, or lack of sexual drive, as also about his hypochondria, preoccupation with fringe doctors and occult ideas. None of Hess's 'peculiarities' were unique, of course, but the ensemble of characteristics made him something of a talking-point. In 1941, some commentators on both the German and British sides would come to regard Hess as having psychotic features (even if for juridical purposes he was, at the end of the day, declared fit to stand trial at Nuremberg). It suited Hitler to use 'mental illness' as an explanation for Hess's flight although again there were differing opinions about how best to present the motives for his departure.

In the early months of Hess's captivity, medical, legal, diplomatic and Intelligence considerations vied for attention. Anxious letters passed between various government ministries and questions were raised in Parliament. Some feared that, should he be declared mad, propaganda advantages might be lost and/or that there might even be calls for his repatriation to Nazi Germany. Others anticipated the possibility that Hess might use 'the insanity plea' in a future trial. In dealing with their patient, British army doctors, such as John Rawlings Rees (medical director of the Tavistock Clinic) and Henry Dicks, thus faced competing agendas and pressures. Due to his family circumstances, Dicks had grown up with fluency in German (as well as Russian). He was able to converse with Hess the most directly. In the to and fro of these sometimes fraught and difficult interactions, Dicks and his colleagues sought to gain a better understanding of the Nazi's 'inner world'. They were not just in search of forensic and diplomatic information (Why had he come? What had he done? Who lay behind his peace mission?) but were also engaged in what they hoped would be a scientific psychological inquiry of wider political and moral interest–an inquiry into Nazi loyalties, fears, desires and fantasies.

The language of the ensuing reports was a strange brew, in parts sounding like a psychoanalytic report, in others like an older Victorian treatise on degeneracy. The case study, when eventually published in 1947, under the editorship of Rees, was said to serve as a political warning for future generations. To study such men, we are told in the preface to the casebook (Rees *et al.* 1947), is important, since the action of a small cabal can unleash catastrophic consequences. There is no space to explore here in any detail the extended encounters that took place between the patient and the doctors, most notably Dicks; suffice to say that, in the face of Hess's claims of amnesia and an array of bizarre symptoms, grievances, and complaints, the clinicians had a bizarre and sometimes torrid time. Mostly they seem to have kept their cool and tried to make some sense of their charge, endeavouring, of course never wholly successfully, to regard him as though he were but an ordinary patient.

From first arrival and throughout his captivity Hess's own reports and claims vied with those of his captors. Hess himself was extremely anxious about his state despite a sometimes insouciant display. On arrival, his pockets were found to be stuffed with homeopathic and nature cure medicines. He was carrying an elixir (apparently for gall bladder troubles) that had been passed to him by Dr Sven Hedin, the Swedish explorer and Nazi sympathizer, who had obtained it from a Tibetan Lamasery. Hess was also carrying a collection of vitamin preparations, glucose and sedatives.

Despite Hess's complaints of ill-treatment and his chronic fears of poisoning and assassination, his guards were not slow to point out the vast discrepancy between the rather benign treatment he was receiving and that meted out by the Nazis to their victims. But Hess was unrepentant. Although suspicious of his interrogators, Hess retained at least one good object, a confidant (whose identity shifted) whom he regarded as kind and trustworthy, amidst a sea of odious officers, whom he often believed to be in a state of hypnosis themselves. The hypnosis was brought on by the Jews. This differentiation amongst his captors, which of course may also have owed a good deal to British interrogation tactics ('good cop/bad cop') was also sometimes interpreted by them at the time as a kind of splitting of his 'objects' into absolute good and evil. The disavowal and projection of all badness into the object was read, in this period, in the light of Freud, but perhaps also obliquely of Klein, whose work had proved so influential in British psychoanalytical circles in and beyond the 1920s. The whole affair was cast in the report as both deadly serious and yet somewhat absurd, even surreal. This persisted from the moment of Hess's arrival through to the Nuremberg trial, where he sat, apparently nonchalantly, reading a novel, in a fog of supposed amnesia, ignoring procedures, smiling mysteriously, then suddenly announcing, to the consternation of his lawyers, that he had recovered his memory after all.

Years before, in Britain, one could be forgiven for thinking that the bizarre atmosphere (a mix of cat and mouse games, old-style gentility, subterfuge, curious gestures?) had invaded the officers guarding Hess as well as Hess himself. What is one to make of the occasional offers of dinner and wine in the officers' mess? Or the country walks and picnics that were occasionally arranged on his behalf in the Welsh hills? Some locals, spotting the German out and about, would incredulously report this to their friends and neighbours, adding further layers to the gathering folklore surrounding the case. The curious undertones of tension and of barely suppressed mirth ran all the way back to the night on which Churchill was briefed about Hess's arrival: the Prime Minister had refused to interrupt a screening of a Marx Brothers comedy before meeting the informant who had come as a matter of the highest priority to meet him. When news of the picnics, walks and other perks seeped out, it led to critical mutterings in the press. In one joke, which did the rounds in some circles in Germany, Churchill was said to have asked Hess: 'So you're the madman, are you?' 'Oh no,' Hess replied, 'only his deputy' (Kershaw 1998, p. 375).

Hess contributed to Rees's published inquiry, despite his obstructionism, even writing a preface for the book. Despite his much debated 'amnesia', his record had always been far from blank. He was a sometimes difficult and sometimes very willing participant. He was given IQ and other tests, asked about his family history and medical records. As the battery of psychological tests unfolded, it was clear that a different kind of clinical observation was also going on – more psychoanalytic in orientation – in which his way of relating to these tests and to his captors as well as to the memory of his family and colleagues back home was monitored. The psychological testing was thus shadowed by a more self-reflective and complex style of quasi-psychoanalytic reporting.

Hess was asked to undertake the Rorschach ink-blot test. He was observed as he underwent it; ditto with the truth drugs that were applied by Dicks (and from which at another level the authorities gleaned very little). Like 'truth serum', which was also applied to Hess, Rorschach tests had been an innovation of the 1920s. The interpreters construed his responses to the blots as indicative of aggressive and violent impulses, tinged with hysteria, but above all found his impoverished associations symptomatic of his 'flat', lifeless quality, his 'vitiated instinctive life' and his psychopathic tendencies. In this inquiry, conducted over several years, a wealth of information emerged not least through the records of his grievances about his maltreatment and his way of relaying those grievances. Observations were made of the hidden world he constructed (for instance, secreting messages around his rooms and under the bed). Behind the scenes, the doctors speculated about the nature of what they called Hess's 'neurotic alibi', and they sought to understand the intricate relationship between his 'inferiority complex', grandiosity, paranoia and hypochondria.

Some faint echo of the 'play technique' that Klein had developed in her psychoanalytic work with young children in the 1920s can perhaps be identified in the wartime observations of Hess's games. Various hypotheses were reached about the symbolic significance of the Nazi's attitudes to his guards, the messages he sent, the letters he wrote and designs he drew. When Hess produced architectural plans for the ideal house of the future, his watchers suspected a manic attempt at reparation. Hess meanwhile claimed to feel no guilt or responsibility; he said he remembered nothing, and anyway attributed 'bad' actions inside Nazi Germany to the sinister hypnosis of gentiles by Jews.

In another section, a few pages later, the report suggests the physicians were indeed conspicuously interested in meanings and in the symbol-filled internal world of Hess, not just in his body and face or his biological history. Here the language sounds more congruent with psychoanalytic, clinical studies of the time, for instance, exploring the unconscious symbolic meanings of play. Thus Hess was found to be 'something of a gadgeteer, who would delight in fantasies of hidden knobs working concealed wirelesses, sliding doors and tricks of illumination' (Rees *et al.* 1947, p. 36).

The authors were interested in the meanings of this play and suggested these would 'not elude the psychopathologist'. Although they did not fully spell out what they thought might be going on inside him, they wondered if: 'This fantasy of his own inviolable home in which he could entertain and shape life exactly as he wanted it was perhaps his best moral support during this phase of his captivity' (Rees *et al.* 1947, p. 36). He created what Dicks *et al.* called a 'dream house', and it was suggested that this was a very egocentric project in which his study and the public reception rooms played a much greater part than his wife's bedroom or his son's nursery. He gave the impression constantly that, though a model family man, he was not in fact greatly interested in his wife as a sexual partner or a love object. If he was caught up in a narcissistic, withdrawn world of his own, this came to be understood in part as an endeavour to find shelter from a host of persecutory threats, including an intolerable storm of persecutory guilt (Rees *et al.* 1947, p. 36).

At the centre of much of the psychoanalytical style of investigation of the Nazi personality was, as mentioned, the superego, that crucial concept formulated by Freud soon after World War I, to describe an unconscious agency of the mind that watches, more or less critically, judgmentally and fantastically, over the ego. Perhaps our familiarity with this language now blunts awareness of just how dramatically innovative a concept the superego had appeared when first elaborated. What marked out Freud's notion of the superego from previous philosophical accounts of 'conscience' was the emphasis on the unconscious dimension: we can feel guilty without knowing it. Moreover, the violent and cruel force of the superego was often seen to be greater than the external prohibitions and demands coming from outside. The subject could be faced, say, by an unpropitious (parental) environment further exacerbated by the unconscious, aggressive drives that coloured that environment and then, in turn, came to be introjected. In a 1926 essay on the superego, Ernest Jones noted how sadistic and persecutory even ordinary (outwardly directed) morality often is. He suggested that in the formation of the super-ego we can see how this turns around upon the subject with all the force of our sadism (Jones 1926).

A number of clinicians in the 1920s and the 1930s observed cases in which the superego operates with vicious severity towards the ego. In obsessional neurosis it inflicts endless self-torment. In melancholia, it fosters 'a pure culture of the death instinct'. The concept of the superego proliferated in many creative ways in Freud's own thought and beyond, notably in the work of Klein. She proposed a different time-line from the one that Freud had set out, pushing an account of the superego much earlier in the life of the infant. Initially Klein had sought to correlate her account with Freud's, but by the 1930s, she was increasingly linking up her own ideas of the superego to Freud's earlier work on the death instinct. In an illuminating article, Edna O'Shaughnessy (1999) describes Klein's picture of a pathological superego that stood apart and was unmodified by the normal processes of growth: in short, an ego-destructive superego. This was a theme taken up by a number of other psychoanalysts after the war such as Wilfred Bion and Herbert Rosenfeld.

To trace the encounter between Fascism and psychoanalysis in the 20th century is in essential respects to trace the history of the application of the idea of the superego. One might also ask here about how far the idea of the superego came to be informed and enriched by the analysis of Fascism. This particular set of concerns was evident in the interaction with Hess during the war. Equally striking, the focus was, to a certain degree at least, the 'here and now'. Instead of concentrating exclusively on the individual's previous political record, interviewers sought to pick up, in gross and subtle forms, something of the unconscious attitude to authority in the present, and to gauge the demands and severity of the subject's punitive attitudes as they came to be transferred on to the current situation. Attitudes to sexuality, to anxiety, to parents and siblings, to violence and destruction, to guilt, reparation and mourning were all to be explored, but the crucial added ingredient was the analysis of the shifting responses and underlying attitudes in the interview itself.

Dicks attempted at one or two points to make certain interpretations to Hess about his own guilt and defences against guilt, for instance, in relation to his anti-Semitism. The Jews' fate, Hess insisted, was brought down upon them by their own malign psychological powers – they had literally hypnotized the Germans into maltreating them. Even when he was confronted with what occurred in concentration camps, Hess insisted the guards must have been unconsciously transfixed by the Jewish inmates to act so improperly, and were thus not responsible. It was, in Dicks's view, a question of Hess's unconscious defensive organization resisting the truth. He told Hess that his explanations were a transparent effort at 'rationalizing' and thus avoiding the unbearable guilt he felt. Hess denied this.

The case book illustrates the very uneven nature of the treatment and theory of the doctors at the time, caught, as it were, between a positivist psychiatry and modern psychoanalysis. In one passage of the report, for instance, we find descriptions reminiscent of Victorian 'alienism', akin to the models of Cesare Lombroso or Henry Maudsley – the face of the criminal a direct signpost to the underlying character – that criminals looked beastly, which was to say closer to lower forms of life (much of this drawn loosely from Darwinian ideas about our animal 'descent'). Thus Hess was portrayed as having a 'full face [that] produced an impression of baleful strength'. His profile 'disclosed a receding forehead, exaggerated supra-orbital ridges covered with thick bushy eyebrows, deeply sunken eyes, irregular teeth which tended to be permanently bared over the lower lip in the manner of "buck" teeth, a very weak chin and receding lower jaw.' In short there was a normative assumption about the face, and Hess's didn't fit it. His ears were 'misshapen and placed too low in relation to the height of the eyes'. His palate was said to be 'narrow and arched'. And as the doctor summed up: 'The whole man produced the impression of a caged great ape, and "oozed" hostility and suspicion.' But at this point an emotion is noted: Hess produced an effect in the group, 'an awkward tense feeling' (Rees *et al.* 1947, pp. 28–9). Here the focus shifted from the visual to the affective, and thereby to questions about unconscious communication between and within people. They considered the way Hess sought to maintain stern and rigid boundaries between good and bad, gentile and Jew, and apparently remained as committed as ever to the Nazi system. He was seen, for all his bizarre features and idiosyncratic form of madness, as an exemplary Nazi. That is to say, he was viewed as in thrall to a cruel and merciless superego, seeking, through his political affiliation, to appease, serve and ingratiate himself with an implacable master, whilst locating all the abjection in the reviled object – the Jew.

V

A few concluding thoughts. In his history of Europe, *Dark Continent: Europe's Twentieth Century*, Mark Mazower (1998) writes critically of the tendency to explain away Fascism, after 1945, as 'a political pathology by which insane dictators led bewitched, hypnotized populations to their doom' (p. xii). 'A funeral oration' [on a culture], he warns, is not tantamount to 'historical analysis'. Mazower goes on: 'The wounds of the continent cannot be dismissed as the work of a few madmen, and its traumas will not be found to lie in the mental condition of Hitler or Stalin' (1998, p. xii). He quotes the following remark from Hannah Arendt: 'We can no longer afford to take that which was good in the past and simply call it our heritage'. She warns against discarding 'the bad' and simply thinking of it as 'a dead load which by itself time will bury in oblivion' (1998, p. xii). Mazower then remarks: 'National socialism, in particular, fits into the mainstream not only of German but also of European history far more comfortably than most people care to admit' (1998, p. xii). I agree, but it seems to me that the historical task also lies in reconstructing the way in which Fascism was understood as political pathology – in short to historicize the discourse that Mazower rejects and to unearth the projects of that other time.

Moreover, in historiography, social theory and psychoanalysis, something of the same insistence on the need to integrate Nazism into accounts of what Mazower calls 'the mainstream' can all be registered. States of mind described in the critical literature on Nazism were not to be seen (so it was argued by various historians and psychoanalysts alike) as entirely alien or as confined to Germany. The fantasies and projections that we can see so flagrantly at work in the Fascist period also raise more fundamental questions about politics at large: remember Freud's own suggestion in the 'Group Psychology' paper that something quite mad may be lurking in, or be a structuring fantasy of, any organized group – an army or a church, for instance, not merely in the delusions of the rampaging 'mob'. Rather, such propensities, that Fascist strain, could be understood as potentially a part of all of us and/or of European culture and thought. The question was then, as it is now, how far there are other forces – or resources – available to counteract rather than to exploit sadism, to contain or lessen, rather than to fan the flames of, collective hatreds or mad idealizations of the avenging 'superego' figure who promises final purification and redemption from the morass. Psychoanalysis offers a rich vocabulary, perhaps partly inspired by those convulsions of history, and certainly a vocabulary that could be used to think about that history. Its concepts should not serve to 'explain away' the wounds of the continent in the 1930s and 1940s as the work of a few madmen, but rather to grasp the unconscious fantasies mobilized in the ideology and practice of Fascism.

A host of further questions could also be put here as to the links between post-war psychological theories, political philosophies and social policies. I wonder how far, for example, visions of psychological fragmentation and integration or the close clinical interest in emotional 'attachment' or, again, attempts to move away from 'authoritarian' models of parenting and education, shaped, or were shaped by, the wider politics of post-war welfarism? What was the connection between endeavours, after 1945, to bring psychoanalysis to bear in the understanding of 'psychopathy' and political and philosophical debate about the psycho-social causes and consequences of Nazism? To what degree did clinical discussion of the patient's 'tolerance' – for instance, of moment by moment shifts in the capacity to make use of 'ego-dystonic' interpretations – echo or amplify contemporaneous social debates about freedom of speech or about insidious anti-democratic organizations? I cannot do more here than signal these questions and refer the reader to the illuminating discussions already published elsewhere, for instance, in Denise Riley's *War in the Nursery* (Riley 1983) and Eli Zaretsky's *Secrets of the Soul* (Zaretsky 2004).

Notwithstanding these excellent studies, much still remains to be investigated as to the influences and reverberations of 20th-century political history and contemporaneous psychological theories about 'what people are like'. But be that as it may, neither the enduring significance of the Third Reich for psychoanalysis, nor the role of Freudian thought in the wider struggle against Fascism can be underestimated.

References

Adorno, T.W. *et al.* (1950) *The Authoritarian Personality*. New York, NY: Harper.

Adorno, T.W. (1951) Freudian theory and the pattern of Fascist propaganda. In: P. Roazen (ed.), *Sigmund Freud*, pp. 82–102. New York, NY: da Capo, 1973.

Cocks, G. (1985) *Psychotherapy in the Third Reich*. Oxford: Oxford University Press.

Dehli, M. (2009) Shaping history: Alexander Mitscherlich and German psychoanalysis after 1945. *Psychoanalysis and History* 11(1): 55–73.

Dicks, H.V. (1972) *Licensed Mass Murder: A Socio-Psychological Study of Some SS Killers*. London: Chatto.

Fermaglich K.L. (2006) *American Dreams and Nazi Nightmares: Early Holocaust Consciousness and Liberal America, 1957–1965*. Waltham, MA: Brandeis University Press; Hanover, NH: University Press of New England.

Freud, A. (1937) *The Ego and the Mechanisms of Defence*. London: Hogarth, 1947.

Gerhardt, U. (ed.) (1993) *Talcott Parsons on National Socialism*. New York, NY: Aldine de Gruyter.

Gilbert, G. (1948) *Nuremberg Diary*. London: Eyre & Spottiswoode.

Goldensohn, L. (2004) *The Nuremberg Interviews*. New York, NY: Knopf.

Jones, E. (1926) The origin and structure of the super-ego. *International Journal of Psychoanalysis* 7: 303–11.

Jung, C.G. (1934) The state of psychotherapy today. *Civilization in Transition. Collected Works*. 2nd edn. vol. 10. Princeton, NJ: Princeton University Press, 1970.

Kershaw, I. (1987) *The Hitler Myth: Image and Reality in the Third Reich*. Oxford: Clarendon.

Kershaw, I. (1998) *Hitler: Nemesis*. London: Penguin.

King, P. (2003) *No Ordinary Psychoanalyst: The Exceptional Contributions of John Rickman*. London: Karnac.

Makari, G. (2008). *Revolution in Mind: The Creation of Psychoanalysis*. London: Duckworth.

Mazower, M. (1998) *Dark Continent: Europe's Twentieth Century*. New York, NY: Knopf.

Mitscherlich, A. & Mitscherlich, M. (1975) *The Inability to Mourn: Principles of Collective Behavior*, preface by Robert Jay Lifton. New York, NY: Grove Press.

O'Grady, J. (2008) The law of unintended consequences: Review of George Makari, *Revolution in Mind. Guardian*, 1 March 2008.

O'Shaughnessy E. (1999) Relating to the superego. *International Journal of Psychoanalysis* 80: 861–70.

Rees, J.R. *et al.* (1947) *The Case of Rudolph Hess: A Problem in Diagnosis and Forensic Psychiatry, by the Physicians in the Services Who Have Been Concerned With Him from 1941 to 1946*. London: Heinemann.

Riley, D. (1983) *War in the Nursery: Theories of the Child and Mother*. London: Virago.

Rosenbaum, R. (1998) *Explaining Hitler*. New York, NY: Random House.

Samuels, A. (1992a) National psychology, national socialism, and analytical psychology: Reflections on Jung and anti-Semitism. Part I. *Journal of Analytical Psychology* 37: 3–28.

Samuels, A. (1992b) National psychology, national socialism, and analytical psychology: Reflections on Jung and anti-Semitism. Part II. *Journal of Analytical Psychology* 37: 127–48.
Shamdasani, S. (2003) *Jung and the Making of Modern Psychology: The Dream of a Science*. Cambridge: Cambridge University Press.
Zaretsky, E. (2004) *Secrets of the Soul: A Social and Cultural History of Psychoanalysis*. New York, NY: Knopf.

ABSTRACT

This paper discusses how psychoanalytic ideas were brought to bear in the Allied struggle against the Third Reich and explores some of the claims that were made about this endeavour. It shows how a variety of studies of Fascist psychopathology, centred on the concept of superego, were mobilized in military intelligence, post-war planning and policy recommendations for 'denazification'. Freud's ideas were sometimes championed by particular army doctors and government planners; at other times they were combined with, or displaced by, competing, psychiatric and psychological forms of treatment and diverse studies of the Fascist 'personality'. This is illustrated through a discussion of the treatment and interpretation of the deputy leader of the Nazi Party, Rudolf Hess, after his arrival in Britain in 1941.

Key words: Fascism, Rudolf Hess, superego

DOI: 10.3366/E1460823509000373

THE DISAPPOINTED OF THE EARTH

Caroline Rooney, Canterbury, UK

The title of this essay, 'The Disappointed of the Earth', alludes to Frantz Fanon's *The Wretched of the Earth*, and what Fanon (1961) may be said to be preoccupied with in this work is the arrested development of humanism on two broad fronts. Firstly, he is critical of the failure of European humanism with respect to the glaring gap between its ideals of universality and the historical existence of colonial oppression. Secondly, he is critical of the ways in which anti-colonial liberation movements are betrayed by a postcolonial nationalism that shrinks and reduces the wider national struggle to the self-maintaining interests of fast-track elites. In both cases, what is at stake is a situation in which forms of ethnic and class elitism make use of an ideology of inclusiveness without the true social and socialist base for such. Fanon may be said to be radically disappointed with the dehumanizing limitations of both European humanism and African nationalism as they betray their own fundamental or founding tenets.

With these questions of failed inclusiveness as regards the human sociality of labour introduced, I wish now to turn to Alaa Al Aswany's Cairo-based novel, *The Yacoubian Building* (Al Aswany 2002), with respect to its attention to the psychological and emotional formations of fundamentalist convictions. What I hope to put forward is a theory of chronic disappointment in relation to something I wish to call 'life abandonment' as a means of trying to account for some of the conditions leading to the sedimentation of extreme beliefs.

In Al Aswany's *The Yacoubian Building*, we are offered an account of a young man's downfall as he is faced with a chain of events that compel his involvement in political and religious extremism. This young man, called Taha, is the son of a doorkeeper in the Yacoubian building which is situated at the hub of downtown Cairo. In the buzzing, teaming heart of this great city, Taha is able to lead only a shadow life since he is forced to take on a

CAROLINE ROONEY is the Director of the Centre for Colonial and Postcolonial Research at the University of Kent. She has published widely on both postcolonial studies and psychoanalysis, and she is currently the principal investigator of an ESRC/AHRC research grant that serves to explore the formations of religious and political extremism. Address for correspondence: School of English, University of Kent, Canterbury, Kent CT2 7NX. [c.r.rooney@kent.ac.uk]

menial existence in which his living humanity is repeatedly not recognized. In order to escape this half-life of constant humiliation, he seeks to elevate himself through applying himself to the schooling and training necessary to gain entry into the Police Academy. His expectations are described in the following terms:

> [H]e beholds himself in his mind's eye as a police officer strutting proudly in his beautiful uniform with the brass stars gleaming on his shoulder [...] He imagines that he has married his sweetheart [...] and that they have moved to a suitable apartment in an up-market district far from the noise and dirt of the roof.
>
> He fervently believed that God would make all his dreams come true. (Al Aswany 2002, p. 20)

Therefore, he has a strongly emotional belief in his betterment in materialistic and class terms as reflective of his true worth and, given that he wishes to make progress through his acceptance into the ranks of the modern middle classes, it would not be possible to posit him as a traditionalist in the face of modernity. This is a point to be taken up a little further on.

At the final interview for Taha's entry into the Police Academy he is turned down due to the fact that his father's low class status is revealed: ironically, while his father is despised as a doorkeeper, the interview panel act as doorkeepers themselves. (With affected refinement the panel call the father 'a property guard', when they may be said to be guardians of the proper and property themselves [Al Aswany 2002, p. 60].) Taha's long years of determined preparation towards his desired self-betterment therefore come to nothing in an instant – a crushing and chronic disappointment. This disappointment is precisely lack of appointment, even categorical unappointability. Because this unappointability has nothing to do with a lack of talent, application and personal qualities on Taha's part, he comes to consider the bourgeois system of appointment as thoroughly inauthentic. In particular, its democratic principles appear to him a sham.

I would now like to cross-reference the chronic disappointment of Al Aswany's Taha with the opening scenes of Herzl's *Old New Land [Alteneuland]*. The opening section of the novel is entitled 'An Educated, Desperate Young Man', and what is striking is that it depicts the condition of young Jewish men in Europe as one of chronic disappointment. This is because, like Taha in *The Yacoubian Building*, these young men are educated and talented but are treated as if they were unappointable. Herzl depicts the constituency of young men he is concerned with in the following terms:

> They were really only a superior kind of proletariat, victims of a viewpoint that had dominated middle-class Jewry twenty or thirty years before: the sons must not be what the fathers had been.... And so the younger generation entered the 'liberal' professions en masse. The result was an unfortunate surplus of trained men who could find no work, but were at the same time spoiled for a

modest way of life. They could not, like their Christian colleagues, slip into public posts... (Herzl 1902, pp. 8–9)

As in *The Yacoubian Building*, what is at stake is a desire for self-betterment. Moreover, this self-betterment is not merely conceived of in materialistic terms but considered to be a matter of spiritual refinement and elevation. In *Old New Land*, the unemployed Friedrich is told by a concerned friend: ' "You let too many things disgust you. One must be able to swallow things [...] Get thee to a nunnery, Ophelia!" ' (Herzl 1902, p. 9). The implication is therefore that Friedrich's desire for self-betterment in class terms is bound up with a squeamish desire for a spiritual purity of being. This is similar to Taha's situation in *The Yacoubian Building* since he seeks to escape the dirt of his father's existence for something cleaner, purer, more refined.

In *The Yacoubian Building*, when Taha fails to obtain a place at the Police Academy, he enrols for a degree at Cairo University. However, he feels tawdry in comparison with those students who are comfortably and securely middle class. For instance, Al Aswany writes: '[W]hen he saw his student colleagues, he discovered that his clothes were not at all what was called for and that the jeans in particular were nothing but a cheap, second-rate imitation of the original' (Al Aswany 2002, p. 90). It is this sense of an inability to break into a social elite that leads to his radicalization through a political and religious movement on his campus.

A panel at a recent conference at Cairo University, 'Egypt at the Cross-roads', addressed the contemporary role of the university within Egypt.[1] In particular, Mohamed Abou-Elghar, who set up the university reform group called 'March 9' five years ago, spoke of how a university education that fails to develop and work with the aspirations of students could lead to students feeling 'totally crushed'. I was struck by the use of this phrase 'totally crushed' since it describes the feeling of chronic disappointment. From the point of view of a novel like *The Yacoubian Building*, students who feel 'totally crushed' in the course of their education seem likely to be drawn to idealistic movements of religious and/or political extremism.

What I am trying to challenge somewhat with respect to this line of argument is the commonplace notion that fundamentalism constitutes a rejection of modernity together with a stubborn, fearful adherence to tradition. Karen Armstrong writes in the Afterword to her study of fundamentalism across different faiths: 'The modern world, which seems so exciting to a liberal, seems Godless, drained of meaning, and even satanic to a fundamentalist'. She continues: 'If a patient brought such paranoid, conspiracy-laden, and vengeful fantasies to a therapist, he or she

---

1. 'Egypt at the Crossroads', Ninth International Symposium on Comparative Literature, Cairo University, 4–6 November 2008. Proceedings forthcoming.

would undoubtedly be diagnosed as disturbed' (Armstrong 2004, p. 368). While Armstrong's multi-faceted study does not always resort to such stark dichotomies, the above comments reflect a too easy or 'shorthand' tendency to posit fundamentalism as an irrational rejection of modernity. What this essay is aiming to broach is how such a position risks a certain blindness to economic and other material conditions together with their psychological effects. In some mitigation of this, attending to the effects of the affect of disappointment may serve to alleviate bewilderment over the formation of extreme beliefs with a means of effective analysis. What is also at stake in such an approach is the understanding that there is a cross-cultural and trans-historical pertinence to the role of chronic disappointment that may serve to prompt reconsiderations of an inclusive humanity in the face of both the desire to *other* extremism along with extremism's own *otherings*.

Al Aswany in an interview speaks of how the character of Taha arose from his acquaintance with young fanatics whom he had come to know through running a seminar for them in downtown Cairo over a 10-year period, and he states: 'I felt that, faced with a certain injustice, anyone could become dangerous, a terrorist because he had lost the dream of his life' (Al Aswany 2008, p. 11).

Zionism and fundamentalism obviously differ with respect to their diverse political and ideological occasions and articulations, while certain developments of Zionism may be considered in terms of fundamentalism. My particular concern is to raise the question of some possible common conditions in the formations of extreme beliefs, especially around questions of disappointment.[2]

It seems to me that, with the fundamentalist tendency in Egypt represented by Al Aswany on the basis of the radicalized young men he has worked with, what is at stake is less a matter of rejecting modernity than one of experiencing its rejections of the self-advancing *parvenus*. It seems also to be a matter of wanting a modernity made good or authentic. Jared Cohen expresses some surprise in his travelogue *Children of Jihad* when he discovers that the young extremists he attempts to fraternize with in the Middle East are into mobile phones, rap music, McDonald's, consumer goods, along with the wearing of veils and the holding of anti-Western sentiments (Cohen 2007, pp. 1–6).[3] It is as if there is an evident desire for modernity at stake but a more authentically moral modernity.

---

2. In writing of hardline supporters of the Jewish state, Ghada Karmi comments: 'Such people, whom I always suspected had probably failed to make adequate lives in their places of origin, or were socially maladjusted, acquired status and a mission in life when they emigrated to Israel [...] they could "act out", to borrow a psychoanalytic phrase, their aggressions, feelings of inferiority or social exclusion' (Karmi 2007, p. 63).

3. For instance, Cohen writes: 'Technology widened the generational gap, affording these youths the opportunity to communicate in new and liberating ways. I found youths of every political persuasion in the Middle East living multiple lives, separating their social and recreational activities from their ideological enterprises' (Cohen 2007, p. 6).

As I have begun to point out, the desire for appointment is given a certain spiritual aura. In relation to this, what is arresting about the actual feeling of disappointment is that it is a feeling of being crushed. I mention this because that crushed feeling is significant for Kant's ethics of the sublime. According to Kant, the sublime affect has distinct phases. At first, the spirit may be raised up in exhilarated identification with what is awesome and elevated. This may then be followed by a reverse movement in which the individual subject feels dwarfed and even rendered utterly insignificant in relation to the experience of the overwhelming immensity or power of the sublime.[4] I would like to propose that there may sometimes be a further, third affective phase to this staggered experience. After first awe, then crushing disappointment or being dashed down, I believe that there can be a further feeling of falsity or inauthenticity. What I am proposing is that the transcendental majesty offered by the sublime may, through the experience of disappointment, be perceived to be false or misleading; it is here that questions of authenticity and inauthenticity may arise.

What Taha's story in *The Yacoubian Building* and the opening of *Old New Land* both serve to suggest is that there may be too much faith – that might be the word to use – in capitalist modernity. In both texts, capitalist modernity is hoped to have the power to cleanse, raise up, sanctify and purify the lowly and dirty. The two texts, however, obviously follow different paths in tackling the consequences of this belief.

In *The Yacoubian Building*, while Taha comes to see the modernity he once had faith in as being corrupt and inauthentic, this would not have occurred if he had not seen modernity as the means of spiritual redemption in the first place. The falsity of his position is that he considers the state of being raised up, elected over others, appointed, chosen, to be a case of spirituality when, surely, it is more accurately a case of narcissism. Furthermore, he may be said to confuse an all-embracing principle with a hierarchical and singling-out one. When he turns to the Islamic fundamentalists on the campus, it is with the force of a transference – which is to say that he seeks to transfer the hopes for appointment to religion. As he comes to be more embroiled in the fundamentalist movement through various events, the leaders of the fundamentalist movement manipulate his desire for appointment. He is led to believe that he is God's chosen person, the appointed and anointed one. In other words, the condition of disappointment becomes in itself a spiritual qualification, a state of being special or being chosen. Or the disappointed condition becomes itself an elitist one. What I am proposing, with respect to terms suggested by Hannah Arendt and subject to elaboration by Gabriel Piterberg (2008) in *The Returns of Zionism*, is that Taha becomes neither simply a *pariah* or

---

4. Kant uses a terminology of 'displeasure' and 'incapacity' in relation to 'unlimited capacity' (Kant 1790, p. 142).

outcast, nor an arriviste *parvenu*, but a kind of default combination of these positions. I would like to name this default position as being that of a *pariah elite*: an elite of pariahs.

A structure of inversion is at stake: where first Taha sought to project spiritual values onto capitalism, in his recoil from this and his increasing turn towards religion he may be said to project the structures of capitalism onto religion. Although this inversion may be considered in terms of the psyche, I first want to propose that both capitalist modernity and religious fundamentalism are not purely opposite formations in that they mirror each other: they constitute a mirrored oppositionalism. This will be explained through considering that both structures may imply a certain principle of what may be termed 'life abandonment'.

Firstly, Taha feels that, as the son of a doorkeeper, he is leading an abandoned life, or one condemned to irrelevance. However, what he does not realize is that the instrumentalizing logic of capitalism is one in which human beings are treated as things while things or commodities are treated as if they were beings. As Marx understood, capitalism relies on this inversion of beings and things, and the energies of labour are used to perpetuate the machine. In short, in terms of the economic, life is an expendable resource in fuelling the capitalist machine. A certain principle of life abandonment is implied, one that Fascism historically took to extreme conclusions. (Karen Armstrong [2004, p. 200], for instance, considers Fascism to be an extreme form of capitalist modernity.) In Fascism, the state war machine, sanctioned by the national father ideal, commands a sacrificial ethos of life abandonment in relation to it.

When Taha turns to religion, the tragic irony is that this does not deliver him his salvation but literally entails his destruction, as he ends up a martyr for his cause. He replaces one capital ideal for another, and in both cases what appears to be required are expectations of life abandonment to the ideal: either the machine as God or else an instrumentalizing religion. That said, there is still something to be said for Taha's confused struggle not to lose faith. I will return to this question of faith in a moment.

While *The Yacoubian Building* may be said to try to make good the disappointing father ideal through religion, *Old New Land* offers its own different version of this. If, in *The Yacoubian Building*, the socially corrupted father ideal stands to be respiritualized, in *Old New Land*, it is the tired old father ideal of the West that stands to be rejuvenated: the old made new.

There is a mythological structure underpinning *Old New Land* that seems to me to be demonstrably similar to the mythological structure underpinning T.S. Eliot's *The Waste Land*. It broadly concerns the fisher-king legend of the ailing paternal leader whose condition is bound up with the infertility of the land, the waste land that needs to be made to bloom again. In Eliot's version, the infertility of the land also signifies a spiritual sterility. In Herzl's novel, the character of Kingscourt allegorically represents a father ideal given over to cynicism and weariness in the context of reified capitalist relations. It is this character who especially stands to be rejuvenated by the young men of the Zionist movement whose project is also given as one of rejuvenating the old land. It is certainly striking how the novel seems strangely to require Kingscourt as a constant witness to the Zionist endeavour, which seems to prove its worth through rehabilitating him by means of stimulating his enthusiasm. On an ideological level the ideal is posited as needing to be brought to life, while on a psychological level this desire seems to be invested with anxieties around the status of masculinity. Interestingly, in Amos Oz's novel *My Michael* it is noted of post-1948 government policies in Israel: 'The government's action was based on ridiculous assumptions – as if the whole of Israel were one great youth movement' (Oz 2001, p. 48).

In both *Old New Land* and *The Yacoubian Building*, the protagonists who are disappointed as pariahs, socio-economically but also in racial terms in *Old New Land*, are also disappointed in their romantic expectations, failing to obtain the women they dream of. The question arises as to whether they may feel inferior as men in various ways. I wish to single out an episode from each text to open out this question.

In *The Yacoubian Building*, when Taha is arrested for his participation in a student rebellion, he has submission forced upon him through torture and rape. In brief, he comes to equate extreme humiliation with being the *object* of the sexual drive, which he considers to be a feminine position of contempt. Beyond this, he more irrationally seeks to confine helpless sexuality and involuntary sexualization to the feminine at the same time that he seeks to restore masculinity to being the gender of purity and spirituality. He does not deny sexuality *per se*; rather, he seeks to align femininity with shamefully exposed sexuality and masculinity with naive, romantic innocence, as if through a psychic disavowal he seeks to make youthful innocence a masculine rather than a feminine trait. In other words, he could be said to suffer from what may be termed gender disappointment, not that he would be able to admit this, especially in the kind of homophobic culture that the novel portrays or presumes, as explored by Joseph Massad (2007) in *Desiring Arabs*.

In *Old New Land*, there is a very strange scene in which Friedrich meets up with the sweetheart of his youth. What is very odd about this scene is that he expresses great surprise that she has aged over the decades while he clearly assumes that he himself has not aged at all. This indicates the possibility of another case of gender disappointment as he struggles in his mind to make masculinity a condition of perpetual youth and femininity a condition of maturity and ageing (a seeming denial of the transition from the femininity of boyhood to the less feminine state of manhood).

While Taha is drawn to become a martyr in *The Yacoubian Building*, this strongly and dramatically contrasts with Herzl's overt depiction of the Zionist movement as one of tenacious survival. However, what is instructive is the material that Gabriel Piterberg puts forward in his case study of Herzl in *The Returns of Zionism*, where he explores Herzl's unease with his masculinity. Piterberg's argument is that Herzl felt the need to make 'Jews acceptable as Western men' (Piterberg 2008, p. 36). Piterberg puts forward Herzl's admiration for Bismarck in Herzl's own words, as follows:

> Bismarck, Herzl thought, knew how to harness the 'stirrings mysterious and undeniable like life itself, which arose out of the unfathomable depths of the folk-soul in response to the dream [of unity]'. He was able to demand great sacrifice from the Germans, who 'joyfully rushed toward unification in war'. (Piterberg 2008, p. 32)

So here there is admiration for life abandonment in order to vivify the ideal. Piterberg also cites Herzl's admiration for the anarchist Ravachol as follows: 'Ravachol has discovered another voluptuousness: the voluptuousness of a great idea and of martyrdom' (Piterberg 2008, p. 35). This masochistic desire for martyrdom is ideologically supposed to be the height of manliness – which seems absurd in that it may be more aligned with the death drive. It might also be asked what kind of father ideal is predicated on the slaughter of the father's sons?

It seems to me from Herzl's terminology that there is a perplexing confusion at stake between what I have been calling 'life abandonment' and what we more commonly refer to as 'self-abandonment'. For the mystics, self-abandonment entails the joyful or blissful experience of abandoning the self to unite with the divine. Less extremely, self-abandon is a term that implies a happy, carefree suspension of self-consciousness. Life abandonment is certainly not this mystical or joyful state but, on the contrary, it is a painful, destructive experience. Herzl's logic, in keeping with those he admires, performs an inversion whereby life rather than the self is given up, and what it is given up to is precisely an idealized principle of collective selfhood.

Finally, I would like to address one further meaning that may be given to appointment, and thereby disappointment, as a means of indicating a reconfiguration of the pariah beyond the pariah elite. The appointment and disappointment that I have been addressing so far involve a vertical and virtual dynamic of being raised up and dashed down, as in a dynamics of the sublime. Distinct from this, there is another sense of appointment as a matter of a synchronized 'meeting with'. When we make appointments it is to meet with each other for a while at an agreed place and at an agreed time. The work of Ayman El-Desouky on 20th-century Egyptian literature draws attention to how certain Egyptian writers are preoccupied with the

workings of what is known as *amāra*.[5] Among the lexical definitions of
amāra considered in this research by Ayman El-Desouky, the following
are particularly suggestive: *amāra* as 'sign or mark to show the way in a
waterless desert'; 'a definite time or place of appointment'; 'evidence of
good faith'. In a sense, you can only *meet with* someone if you are on a
level with them: avoiding hierarchy because you are on the same level and
avoiding deception because you are on a level, interacting in good faith. If
there is a sense of falseness involved in the sublime, it could well concern the
misplaced hope of finding unity on high. It is a question of what constitutes
'evidence of good faith'.

In the context of addressing the violence that religious fanaticism on
all sides has been unleashed in Lebanon, Jean Said Makdisi makes an
important statement. She writes:

> The worst danger of all, into this bloodbath into which we have been plunged, is
> not the loss of life, but the loss of faith. I don't mean loss of faith in God: I mean
> loss of faith in humanity and each other. (Makdisi 1990, p. 142)

What I want to say in relation to this is that the real lack of appointment
entailed in chronic disappointment is probably, most fundamentally, the loss
of faith in humanity, meaning the loss of faith in our ability to meet with
each other. It is important to clarify this. The faith in humanity in question
is not a question of the triumphant ideal of a proud secular humanism or a
man ideal made good. Not this abstract form of value, it is rather a spiritual
maintaining faith with each other outside any ideology, creed, set of ideals.
And I think that what I am calling the elite pariah or pariah elites is a matter
of formations that conversely arise through the radical distrust of others
in that chronic disappointment certainly serves to foster radical distrust.
For that reason, it seems important to affirm a universality of the pariah,
as may be traced from Lazare to Arendt to Piterberg, and as would entail
sympathies or meeting places amongst the disappointed of the earth.

I began this essay with an invocation of Fanon's *Wretched of the Earth* and
would, in conclusion, like to address a little further how an understanding
of colonial/postcolonial struggles and their attendant liberation/postcolonial
theories may lead us to grasp the significance of chronic disappointment in
a wider historical perspective. What is at stake here is both the authoritarianism of racist settler societies as well as the authoritarian nationalism of
the regimes that emerge in the post-colony.

First of all, the concept of a pariah elite has pertinence in a consideration
of certain aspects of settler societies. Octave Mannoni (1956) has addressed
the psychological inferiority complex of *the settler* (as opposed to native)
in psychological terms, while what is surely also at stake is a sense of

---

5. This work was presented at the 'Egypt at the Crossroads' Conference, Cairo
University, November 2008.

class inferiority, something much overlooked in the analyses of colonialism that are driven by the racial and ethnic givens of identity politics. More specifically, the authoritarian racism of settler societies yet stands to be explored in terms of the forms of chronic disappointment that may have contributed to the compensatory ethos of the settler class as a pariah elite. In *apartheid* South Africa, for instance, the ethos of right-wing nationalism could be partially explained in terms of the Afrikaners' sense of themselves as an outcast group, both displaced from European origins with their hegemonies, as well as snobbishly despised and humiliated by the British within South Africa (especially in the Boer war and its aftermath). This Afrikaans or Boer constituency could certainly be accounted for in terms of pariah elitism, one marked by a distrust of the rest of humanity (the apartness of what came to be *apartheid*). Moreover these settlers came to demarcate themselves precisely and explicitly as a *chosen* people.

It is a certain familiarity with pariah elitism in a Southern African context that has prompted me to try and link the condition in question with aspects of what is sometimes considered to have led Zionism in the direction of an Israeli form of apartheid. Joseph Massad has argued that Jews who were *inferiorized* in Europe came to re-position themselves as rendered *superior* by their Europeanization in their appointed destiny of a return to Israel. Massad writes:

> The solution seemed self-evident: Zionism, in Herzl's words, would set up a state for the Jews that would constitute 'the portion of a rampart of Europe against Asia, an outpost of civilisation as opposed to barbarism.' This state, as Herzl's novel *Alteneuland* uncovered, would outdo the Europeans at their own game of civilisation. The settler colony was going to be the space of Jewish transformation. To become European, the Jews must exit Europe. They could return to it and become part of it by emulating its culture at a geographical remove. If Jews were Asians in Europe, in Asia, they will become Europeans. (Massad 2006, p. 168)

However, what blocks the envisaged dialectical assimilation – 'they could return to it [Europe] and become part of it' – is precisely 'the geographical remove' which is also very much a *psycho*-geographical remove or a question of separatism, this question of separatism being also a feature of fundamentalist movements (in fact, it seems to be paradoxically the trait in common across different forms of fundamentalism). If Israel considers itself as 'an outpost of civilisation', much in the manner of apartheid South Africa, this is not a case of bringing civilization to the natives (the usual colonial excuse, well-meant or not) but instead a messianic matter of saving, preserving or redeeming civilization. But saving it from what? Surely 'the natives' would not constitute an adequate answer here. If saving civilization is at stake, why deliberately take it to locations and situations that threaten it? Rather, it would seem to be a case of saving civilization from *what is barbaric in itself*: in this context, the barbaric would concern the treatment that Jews received from 'civilized' Europeans. So, could the very necessity of the psycho-geographical remove (maintained against any future assimilation) be explained in terms of the elect destiny of *saving Europe from Europe*, that is, from its all too disappointing exposures and shame? This need to remove Europe from itself would require both a safe distance from Europe and a certain defensive 'encystment' of Europe elsewhere.

Aimé Césaire (1993) puts forward the argument that colonialism serves as a safety valve in that Europe uses its colonies to export its barbaric elements, that is, its difficult subjects given over to sadistic, bullying tendencies. But does it not also export its idealism or the desire for a purity that decadent capitalist modernity progressively compromises? [6] If Fascism is colonialism returned to Europe, as Césaire suggests, it manifests itself in an ideology of a *very pure* father ideal that has to be separated from its shamefulness in order to survive.

Returning to questions of Zionism, it is not just the Palestinians that occasion Israeli distrust but far more broadly an untrustworthy humanity. In fact, Avigail Arbarbanel has recently written a moving and perceptive account of this radical distrust of humanity from an Israeli point of view. She writes:

> Growing up as an Israeli provided me with an intimate understanding of Israeli–Jewish psychology. Ever since I can remember, we in Israel were told that Jews have nowhere to go because the world didn't like Jews [...] The idea that Israel is the only safe place for Jews is critical to understanding the roots of the Palestinian–Israeli conflict, and Israel's policies and perspectives in the present. The majority of Jewish people do not trust non-Jewish people as life-long compatriots. (Arbarbanel 2008)

I presume Arbarbanel means Israeli Jews in speaking of the 'majority' in the above. The occasion of her writing this article is her emigration from Israel in order to negate the stance of distrust she addresses. A most visible manifestation of the distrust of humanity in Israel is evident in the creation of 'the security wall' or 'the iron wall' between Israel and its Palestinian neighbours. As Glenn Bowman (2007) has commented, the phenomenon of walling in Israel creates a concretization of a logic of encystation. It may be suggested that, on the one hand, the Palestinians may come to stand in for *the evil of Europe*. That is, they may be in the position of being forced to stand for not only the new Jews but the Nazis reincarnated. At the same time, on the other hand, Israel's encysted self-enclosure may be psychologically understood in terms of a desire to preserve the good that remains of humanity. It can be with an emotional sincerity – and not cynicism – that Israelis protest their innocence, or what can sometimes be

---

6. I try to explore some of this ethos in 'Narratives of South African farms' (Rooney 2005).

heard as bewilderment at the criticism of the Zionist project.[7] Perhaps this confused sincerity becomes less strange if understood in terms of a deeply invested mission to save (European) humanity from its own inhumanity, including *knowledge* of it? Would this mean that what may be encrypted within a certain Israeli psyche is a refusal to mourn, specifically, a refusal to mourn a chronically disappointing, barbarically behaved *Europe*?[8] In addition, it would be pertinent to reflect psychoanalytically on the question of a Western complicity with such a position.

Jean Said Makdisi writes of American perceptions of Israel: 'In this representation, there was confusion between Arab demands for justice and Nazi persecution of the Jews; *civilisation itself was seen as having been rescued by the gallant Israeli army*, as though in some mysterious way it had retroactively undone history' (Makdisi 1990, p. 128, my emphasis). That is, American support for Israel could be construed of in terms of a retroactive wish to erase the Holocaust – a would-be redemptive undoing (as opposed to recognition) of that history, saving civilization from (knowledge of) its barbarity. Might there be a certain Western–Israeli complicity in this protective mythology of 'saving civilization' *from itself*?

While Israel necessarily stands to be understood in terms of settler colonialism, as Piterberg and Massad convincingly argue, the defence of the Jewish return to Israel also obviously draws on a postcolonial logic in some respects: that is, in terms of retrieving a land of which you have been historically dispossessed. The reason this is mentioned is that it may be noted that the category of pariah elite is interestingly one that cuts across the polarity of foreign settler/native restitution.

While the role of chronic disappointment in the establishment of the settler stands to be adequately recognized, what has also been insufficiently grasped is how the 'comprador elite' of newly established dictatorial African post-colonies is not just a *bourgeois* elite, but, more exactly, I would argue, a *pariah* elite. It is as if Fanon's *Black Skin, White Masks* (Fanon 1952), a work that confronts the internalization of the inferiorizing mechanisms of racism, needs to be re-positioned and re-worked as a sequel to *The Wretched of the Earth*.

Zimbabwean writers such as Yvonne Vera (1998) and Tsitsi Dangarembga (2006a, 2006b) have examined in observant detail how settler colonialism with its enticements of accelerated modernity and its lure of self-betterment engenders a structure of expectation in the colonized subject that often turns out to be bitterly thwarted. In particular, Dangarembga, in her two novels towards her planned trilogy, may be read as retrospectively accounting for the genesis of a culture of authoritarian

---

7. Certainly Howard Jacobson in his columns for *The Independent* voices his bewilderment over such criticism.

8. Yolanda Gampel's work takes such questions into account.

nationalism in contemporary Zimbabwe. In both *Nervous Conditions* and *The Book of Not*, the central protagonist desperately struggles to acquire the upward social mobility and, notably, 'cleanliness' that presents itself through the seductions of a colonial modernity being extended to the colonized. Her deeply invested struggle to improve her status is, however, impeded by a number of crushing disappointments: a series of Nots. By the end of *The Book of Not*, these defeats lead her to withdraw into a proud and self-pitying isolation.

Dangarembga's protagonist is from the same kind of social and educational background as the ruling elite in Zimbabwe, that is to say, a class subject to a combination of both pariah and *parvenu* status. Might not Mugabe's stance of go-it-alone resentful arrogance against the West be traceable to his chronic disappointments (he has spoken repeatedly even obsessively of the West as having let him down), this leading to his evident stance as an elite pariah? On the one hand, Mugabe may be considered justified in his sense of disappointment, for instance, over the failure of the Labour government to honour the terms of Lancaster House agreement. On the other hand, he may also be said to use his disappointment in the West to deflect from the fact that he himself is widely considered to be a disappointment.[9] His position as disdainful pariah is certainly one consolidated by the Western media.

The further point to be made with respect to Dangarembga's work is that it links the question of chronic disappointment to gender disappointment. Since the protagonist perceives that males are more socially valued than females, she appears to suffer from gender disappointment. The symptom of it is displaced onto another female character who develops anorexia, where anorexia may be understood as a clinging to the androgynous boyishness of childhood. If anorexia is a symptom of female gender disappointment, the novels by Herzl and Al Aswany analysed earlier give evidence of male gender disappointment with respect to a clinging to the girlishness or youth of male childhood. The problem is not with the gender disappointment itself, which may be due to all kinds of factors including a reluctance to conform to gendered stereotypes, but with the way in which gender disappointment is impossible to confront in homophobic, conventional environments and also difficult to confront because of the resistances of the ego. As such it would be repressed, which may predispose the subject to a neurotic inability to accept and work through future disappointments. It may be briefly noted that the social alienation of the mentally disturbed protagonist of Oz's *My Michael* is secretly haunted by her own case of gender disappointment. For instance: 'When I was nine I used to wish I could grow up as a man instead of a woman' (Oz 2001, p. 5).

---

9. If you google 'Mugabe' an adjective often coupled with his name is 'disappointing'.

The above brief generalizations and broad suggestions have been risked in order to propose how a theorization of chronic disappointment might facilitate a cutting across the rigid formulations, allegiances and counter-allegiances of identity politics towards an understanding of what is both a psycho-affective and socio-economic human condition. As a human condition, it is that which may affect both colonizer and colonized, even as they are differentially spaced in accordance with a psychological and historical awareness of oppressor as possibly once victim and victim as potential oppressor, each vulnerable to the formations and counter-formations of fanaticism.

Theories of mimetic identification are often and widely used to account for the abused coming to resemble those who abuse them. Apart and distinct from such considerations would be the taking into account of this 'counter-mimetic' cycle, one of chronic disappointment and its redemptive or compensatory counter-identifications in the formation of pariah-elite separatisms, for which I have tried to make a propositional case in this essay. What emerges is that all those who would transform their chronic disappointments into cases of 'specialness', 'apartness' or 'appointment' look less like special cases.

The variously maintained notions of being God's chosen would of course require much closer attention. As a preliminary observation, this spiritual vocation is crucially subject to different phases. While it may arise as an outcast and exilic ethical response to inauthentic forms of universality, it becomes problematic when posited as an ethnic or national destiny. What I am suggesting with this line of analysis is that it is *potentially* irrational and dangerous to attempt to configure the religiously or spiritually utopian in terms of an ethnic or national identity.

It would seem to be the redemptive promise of the ideal that is bound to fail, time and again – a messianic structure intrinsic not only to forms of religion but, as put forward by Jacques Derrida (1994) in *Spectres of Marx*, intrinsic also to capitalism. Furthermore, it seems that Freud's version of the ideal, the father ideal, is that it performs a necessarily disappointing role rather than offering a promise of redemption. Jacqueline Rose in tracing the palimpsest of allegiances in the work of Elisabeth Roudinesco significantly and deftly shows how an appreciation of the mysticism of de Certeau augments an affirmation of the need for what Freud posits as the unconscious.[10] In particular, what seems to be at stake is a recognition of the unrequited nature of desire, that is to say, its indissociability from disappointment. In tandem with the necessity of reckoning with disappointment is the need to retain the question of meeting

---

10. I refer to Jacqueline Rose's 'Response to Elizabeth Roudinesco', delivered at the Conference on Psychoanalysis, Fascism and Fundamentalism, London, November 2008 (see pp. 267–8).

up with each other in good faith as a receptive predisposition and as an other-relating praxis without prescriptions. That is, these are not two contrary positions – disappointment and good faith – but positions that may be understood to imply each other. It is, after all, a psychoanalytic insight that an acceptance of our lacks, limitations and vulnerabilities is what enables an opening out towards others, that is, as a relational and emotional possibility and practice as opposed to a philosophically posited abstract ideal of the universal.

References

Al Aswany, A. (2002) *The Yacoubian Building*, trans. H. Davies. London: Harper Perennial, 2007.

Al Aswany, A. (2008) Interview with Maya Jaggi. *Guardian Review*, 23 August 2008.

Arbarbanel, A. (2008) A change needs to come. In: *The Electronic Intifada*, 26 May 2008 [accessed 1 March 2009]. Available from: http://electronicintifada.net/v2/article9567.shtml/

Armstrong, K. (2004) *The Battle for God: Fundamentalism in Judaism, Christianity and Islam*. London: Harper Perennial.

Bowman, G. (2007) Israel's wall and the logic of encystation. *Focaal* 50: 127–36, Dec.

Césaire, A. (1993) Discourse on colonialism. In: P. Williams and L. Chrisman (eds), *Colonial Discourse and Post-Colonial Theory: A Reader*, pp. 172–80. Harlow: Pearson Education.

Cohen, J. (2007) *Children of Jihad: A Young American's Travels Among the Youth of the Middle East*. New York, NY: Gotham Books.

Dangarembga, T. (2006a) *Nervous Conditions*. Banbury: Ayebia Clarke.

Dangarembga, T. (2006b) *The Book of Not*. Banbury: Ayebia Clarke.

Derrida, J. (1994) *Spectres of Marx*, trans. P. Kamuf. London, New York, NY: Routledge.

Fanon, F. (1952) *Black Skin, White Masks*, trans. C.L. Markmann. London: Pluto Press, 1986.

Fanon, F. (1961) *The Wretched of the Earth*, trans. C. Farrington. Harmondsworth: Penguin, 1990.

Herzl, T. (1902) *Old New Land [Alteneuland]*. Minneapolis, MN: Filiquarian Publishing, 2007.

Kant, I. (1790) *Critique of the Power of Judgement*, ed. P. Guyer, trans. P. Guyer and E. Matthews. Cambridge: Cambridge University Press, 2000.

Karmi, G. (2007) *Married to Another Man: Israel's Dilemma in Palestine*. London: Pluto Press.

Makdisi, J.S. (1990) *Beirut Fragments: A War Memoir*. New York, NY: Persea Books.

Mannoni, O. (1956) *Prospero and Caliban: The Psychology of Colonization*, trans. P. Powesland. London: Methuen.

Massad, J.A. (2006) *The Persistence of the Palestinian Question: Essays on Zionism and the Palestinians*. London, New York, NY: Routledge.

Massad, J.A. (2007) *Desiring Arabs*. Chicago, IL: University of Chicago Press.

Oz, A. (2001) *My Michael*, trans. N. de Lange. London: Vintage.

Piterberg, G. (2008) *The Returns of Zionism: Myths, Politics and Scholarship in Israel*. London: Verso.

Rooney, C. (2005) Narratives of Southern African farms. *Third World Quarterly* 26(3): 431–40.

Vera, Y. (1998) *Butterfly Burning*. Harare: Baobab Books.

ABSTRACT

This essay offers a consideration of how the affect of chronic disappointment contributes to the formation of extreme beliefs. It debates how the disappointment in question is a matter of social class and the desire for self-betterment, contesting the assumption that fundamentalism constitutes a simple rejection of modernity. The essay also attempts to theorize the ways in which chronic disappointment can lead to the establishment of what is formulated in terms of 'pariah elitism'. In moving from a consideration of Al Aswany's *The Yacoubian Building* and Herzl's *Alteneuland* to a consideration of colonial and postcolonial situations in Southern Africa, it broaches the question of how chronic disappointment serves to challenge both the othering of extremism and extremism's otherings. Finally, the essay suggests that there is a distinction to be maintained between the idealism of extremism and a praxis of good faith.

Key words: disappointment, pariah, fundamentalism, distrust, faith

DOI: 10.3366/E1460823509000385

THE IMPACT OF ISLAMOPHOBIA

M. Fakhry Davids, London, UK

Islamophobia Today

In the major Western democracies Muslims live as minority communities and are subject to the same out-group prejudice that usually confronts such groups. In these countries there is a general public awareness of the dangers of racism and xenophobia. However, racism can be a slippery phenomenon, and the fact that the Holocaust and colonialism have enjoyed public prominence in the years following World War II can serve to restrict awareness of racism as a problem to another time and place – for example, Germany in a bygone era – leading to unwitting complacency about it in the here-and-now. In the 1990s, the Runnymede Trust published a report that successfully highlighted the existence of anti-Semitism in contemporary Britain, followed by a parallel report some years later outlining discriminatory practices faced by Muslims in the country (Runnymede Trust 1997). Unlike Jews, Muslims are an ethnically diverse group and do not form a homogeneous race, but on examination it became abundantly clear that the processes involved in Islamophobia are in fact those of racism (Seabrook 2004; Sheridan 2002). This bore out Edward Said's observation that:

> Malicious generalisations about Islam have become the last acceptable form of denigration of foreign culture in the West; what is said about the Muslim mind, or character, or religion, or culture as a whole cannot now be said in mainstream discussion about Africans, Jews, or other Orientals, or Asians. (Said 1997, p. xii)

Occasionally an incident does flare up in the public domain that can be seen as symptomatic of this background of intolerance and hostility towards Islam and Muslims. For example, in Paris on 18 September 1989:

> Leila Achaboun, Fatima Achaboun and Samira Saidani – three schoolgirls of North African descent – were suspended from College ... for refusing to remove the headscarves that they understood to be prescribed by Islamic tradition.

M. FAKHRY DAVIDS is a Fellow of the Institute of Psychoanalysis in full-time psychoanalytic practice in London. He has a long-standing interest in the psychology of racism, and has a book on internal racism scheduled for publication in late 2009. Address for correspondence: 4 Primrose Gardens, London NW3 4TJ. [fakhry@bigfoot.com]

> The school's principal ... claimed to be acting in accordance with ... legislation, which prohibited the wearing of religious or political symbols ...
>
> The incident was brought to the attention of Lionel Jospin, then Minister of Education, who overturned [the] decision ..., insisting that, although the French school system should discourage the wearing of the *hidjeb*, it had no right to exclude the girls on that basis... (Blank 1999, p. 537)

Jospin's decision was subsequently upheld by the courts. The French education system is, by law, secular and the visible presence of the headscarf, denoting adherence to Muslim belief, clearly undermines this. On this occasion, however, it was regarded as an anomaly that met a measured response – it was regrettable and to be discouraged. In the hotly contested matter of whether or not to wear a scarf, the Muslim girl was left free to take her own position without placing her education at risk. As a citizen, her right to the mental space in which to grapple with the complex issues involved in such a decision, free from state interference, was upheld. That was 1989, 12 years before the cataclysmic 9/11 attacks on targets in the United States.

In February 2004, nearly 15 years later, the French parliament enacted, by an overwhelming majority,[1] a law that closed this loophole in interpretation. Henceforth, all dress in schools denoting religious affiliation was to be explicitly outlawed: the headscarf, along with the Jewish *kippah*, 'large' Christian crucifixes and the like are now all forbidden. Framed in this way, the law would appear to address religion in general, yet it was widely acknowledged as aimed specifically at Muslims (e.g. Stuttaford 2004) – the others had to be included to uphold the illusion of equality under the law. This was necessary to obscure just how extraordinary an attack it is on civil liberty, one of the hard-won cornerstones of contemporary Western life. The legislation was no less than a systematic, institutionalized assault not on those values themselves, but on the right of the ordinary Muslim to enjoy them. Such assaults call on the formidable power of the state to reach deep into the victim's life, entrapping her in order to ensure that the attack hits home: henceforth the Muslim girl has to choose between an education and her beloved religion. The assertion that it is a measure not against Islam but against religion *in general* is a further blow in that it denies this experience. Psychically, the brutality of this assault matches that of its mirror image, the enforced imposition of the *chador* in the Taliban state – a measure that provoked an outpouring of sympathy in the West for the plight of the hapless Muslim woman.

The French legislation can be seen as the culmination, the final institutionalization, of a wave of violence against Muslims that swept

---

1. 'With opinion polls showing 70 percent approval, the new law swept through the national assembly by 494–36 in February, and then, a month later, was approved 276–20 in the senate. The new rules will come into force from the beginning of the school year in September' (Stuttaford 2004).

Europe following the events of 9/11 (Allen 2002; Allen & Nielsen 2002; Bunglawala 2002, 2004; MCB 2002; Whitaker 2002). Across the Union it became open season on Muslims; just to look like one was to invite attack, as some turbaned Sikhs found to their cost. In the UK, the EU Monitoring Centre on Racism and Xenophobia reported:

> A significant rise in attacks on Muslims ... Numbers of incidents of violent assault, verbal abuse and attacks on property were noted, some ... very serious. Muslim women wearing the hijab were easily identifiable and widespread targets for verbal abuse, being spat upon, having their hijab torn from them and being physically assaulted. A number of prominent mosques around the country were similarly attacked, ranging from minor vandalism and graffiti to serious damage through arson and firebombs.[2] Threatening and explicitly Islamophobic messages were also widely circulated over the Internet and through e-mails. [Abusive] telephone calls, anonymous post and threatening messages left on car windscreens were observed.
>
> ... A disproportionate amount of [media] coverage was devoted to extremist Muslim groups and [individuals willing] to join an Islamic war against the West ... less sensationalist ... voices were mainly overlooked. Reporting included very basic Islamophobic stereotypes shaping the popular image of young British Muslim men. ... The far-right British National Party launched a highly explicit Islamophobic campaign [asserting that] Christianity [was] under threat from Muslims in the UK. (Allen & Nielsen 2002, p. 29)

This general pattern of intolerance occurred across Europe. In Italy, the Prime Minister also famously weighed in with a broadside against Muslim civilization as a whole as backward and intrinsically inferior. Although political correctness later forced a retraction, an increase in the *public expression* of anti-Muslim hatred and xenophobia was nonetheless recorded in Italy. Across the EU, Muslims found themselves held responsible for the events of 9/11, and even bringing this fact into the open – e.g. by publishing opinion poll findings – led to an increase in explicit death and bomb threats against Muslims (Allen & Nielsen 2002, p. 22).

There are many painful and moving examples that, for the sake of brevity, I must pass over. These come from virtually every walk of life and cover systematic harassment, arbitrary physical and psychological assault, as well as persecution, trial, conviction and punishment by suspicion in general (Allen 2002; MCB 2002), and discriminatory treatment by the legal apparatus in particular (Bunglawala 2004). Taken together, they underline the fact that today's Muslim must not expect to be seen as 'one of us'. Instead, he/she is constantly under suspicion; and to be suspected

---

2. In Devon a mosque was desecrated by 'throwing around a number of pigs' heads, red paint to look like blood ... [and by] an offensive banner which ended in the words "Nuck [sic] em George"' (Ahmed 2002, p. 189). The pig is considered unclean in Islamic law, its consumption forbidden.

is to be swiftly punished, the matter of guilt or innocence an academic afterthought.[3]

This brief description alerts us to two aspects of Islamophobia. First, that in Western societies there is a constant but largely invisible level of everyday out-group prejudice directed at Muslims. Later in this paper I shall consider the impact this has on individual development and the role it might play in the attraction of the idea of Islam as radically anti-Western, especially during adolescence. Second, following 9/11 there has been an acute intensification of these trends, which I want to consider briefly as I think it unleashes powerful psychological forces that influence the way we approach and perceive the topic of Islamic fundamentalism.

9/11: The Role of Internal Racism

What light, then, can psychoanalysis shed on what goes on in the mind when the Muslim is vilified as the enemy of the public good in the way that I have been describing?

From the outset psychoanalysts have recognized that racism invokes an us–them divide across which projections can be lodged very effectively – that is, at a distance from the subject. To the extent that projected content is unwanted internally, its projection creates in the outside world a potentially dangerous object whose threats must be constantly anticipated and monitored. The relationship between subject and object is thus inscribed in a paranoid frame which, we might note, will make it difficult to see the true nature of that object – to see them as they really are.

Based on further clinical study of internal racism I have suggested that it involves not an isolated paranoid projection but an organized set of defences that operates in the way theorized by John Steiner (1987) in his concept of the pathological organization. This is a technical distinction that flows from the discovery that disturbed patients tend to employ highly organized systems of defence to shield themselves from inner danger. We can think of these as belonging to an elaborate phantasy system – akin to a parallel dream world – which the patient inhabits psychically, and which is thus credited with protecting him or her. Protection comes, therefore, not from constant and active projection but from unswerving loyalty to a system, which must be constantly serviced. Usually, such defensive organizations are associated with severe psychopathology, but, as we know, racism occurs universally, not just in very disturbed individuals. To account for this we need to introduce the paradoxical idea of a normal pathological

---

3. Recently, newspapers reported that a suspected British terrorist – wanted in connection with an investigation into a terrorist incident in the UK – was killed in a bombing raid in Pakistan (The Observer, 23 November 2008).

organization,[4] an entity that, like its truly pathological counterpart, defends tenaciously against intense anxiety by installing a paranoid view of the situation and then working to insist that this view is the way things really are. In a racist mindset we remain convinced that our prejudiced view of the object is true, to the extent that contrary facts are assimilated in a way that, in essence, confirms that view. Like the pathological organization, it is capable of endless permutations and is highly resistant to change.

To avoid confusion I use the term racist rather than pathological for the normal variant. This is not an accurate term as I want to convey the fact that the object – the target of projections – is usually a member of a socially-sanctioned out-group, and the mechanisms I am describing can be deployed across any divide by which that other is defined, including race, class, language, religion, etc. I use the term racist since I can find no better term that, in our present world, carries the many shades of meaning – ranging from subtle everyday prejudice and dehumanization of the other all the way through to arbitrary racist murder – that can characterize the transactions between subject and object in such organizations. The fact that members of a socially-sanctioned out-group are recruited into this inner structure allows the individual to avoid personal responsibility for what he/she does to the object in their own mind.

In 'The internal racist' (Davids 2003), I gave the example of a brown-skinned, 4 year-old who came to see his skin as dirty to illustrate how these dynamics work in the normal mind. Without much preparation, he had been moved from the class of a much-loved teacher and I showed that he had projected mental dirt – the unbearable affect associated with losing his object – into his skin, and he appealed to his mother to wash him clean and thus rid him of this unwelcome baggage. Darker-skinned people were members of the out-group in his white-majority world, but I found that we could prevent the institutionalization of this racist solution to his emotional difficulty by attending to the underlying separation anxiety. In time, his skin colour became detoxified and he could draw himself once more as brown. Through this example I was able to observe how a racist organization is a normal developmental achievement which, once used, is subsequently available to the individual as a resource with which to manage overwhelming anxiety. Henceforth the child, and later the adult, will never again have to experience the most feared situations associated with infantile helplessness; before reaching that point a racist organization will kick in and present a solution. Following this, rather than being terrified of unknown danger beyond one's control, one will have a known quarry that can be engaged in one way or another. As a paranoid solution it protects, but it

---

4. Freud (1922) posited normal variants of pathological entities encountered in the consulting room, such as 'normal jealousy'; he also viewed religion as a 'normal' neurosis.

does so at the cost of interfering with our ability to get to grips with the real danger.

A striking example of the way in which internal racist functioning came to the rescue can be found in reactions to the 9/11 atrocity. In its immediate aftermath – before evidence as to the identity of those responsible was available, and before the name 'Al-Qā'idah' was in circulation – a notion took hold in the popular imagination that Islamic fundamentalists or terrorists were responsible. This paranoid construction protects us all from the fear of annihilation, which the 9/11 attacks (and again the 7/7/2005 ones here in London) brought forcibly to the surface. Once in place, the experience of being terrorized was projected into the Muslim who, at any moment, might be picked upon, hounded, attacked. While this frees the non-Muslim of the terror of annihilation, the Muslim is, as regular citizen, a target of the terrorist's blunt but deadly weapon and, as Muslim, of his or her fellow citizen's retaliatory psychological response to it. Linking the terms 'terrorist' and 'fundamentalist' with 'Islamic' draws on anti-Islamic sentiment prevalent within Western culture at large (Said 1997), yoking them together in a paranoid construction that identifies the Muslim as enemy. To sustain this belief in the face of contrary facts, Islam must be seen to have something that sets it apart from other religions. I am suggesting that the notion that it has a fundamentalist core fulfils this function.

Using a racist organization to defend against anxiety is not cost-free; its by-product is unconscious guilt about what one does to innocent bystanders who, because they share some features with the Arab/Muslim attackers, have been arbitrarily singled out as the enemy. This is compounded by the problem of triumphalism (Segal 2003): once we realize it is possible to get rid of anxiety in this way, we can become addicted to it, gaining pleasure from inflicting on others suffering that we feel increasingly remote from until, eventually, we triumph over suffering itself. Guilt threatens retaliation by the superego, which further consolidates the organization's grip. The more we use a racist organization to protect us, therefore, the more anxiety we generate; the more anxious we become the more desperately we feel in need of the organization's defences. The work of the organization, which constantly redoubles its efforts to prove Islam's culpability, is thus extensive and relentless, a process into which the media are visibly recruited. However, it can also interfere with our own well-intentioned attempts to arrive at an accurate account of the place of 'fundamentalism' in Islam and thus in the mind of the Muslim.

Islamophobia and Fundamentalism: A Clinical Account

Concreteness is a central feature of fundamentalist states of mind observed in the consulting room, and is usually associated with an early developmental arrest that has prevented movement towards a symbolic level of functioning. It tends to be associated with a failure to progress fully from a psychotic organization of experience to a more normal–neurotic one, a finding borne out by detailed clinical accounts that show what difficult and complex work is required to remedy the situation.

In its popular usage, the notion of Islamic fundamentalism refers to a state of mind that appears, on the surface, to be characterized by the same quality of concreteness and lack of symbolism. In common with the fundamentalist approach in other religions (Summers 2006) scriptural injunctions are viewed in a literal rather than symbolic way – the Qur'anic injunction that women must cover themselves in public, for instance, cannot be interpreted to mean modesty in dress. The literalist view also tends towards intolerance of other viewpoints, a stance that emanates from a moral high ground: close to the Word means closer to God and hence superior, which elides easily into the only correct and acceptable way. As in most religions, the literalist view is one of many, and the process by which it is transformed into the only one tolerated is a complex one that is under-investigated and in need of further illumination. However, since the Qur'an is believed to be the literal word of God transmitted directly to the Prophet Muhammad, this can give rise to the idea that concrete, literal truth occupies a more central position in Islam than it does in other religions. In an Islamophobic mindset this can be seen as proof that Islam as a religion has a fundamentalist core.

In fact, of course, in Islamic theology at large, diversity of interpretation is valued – the Prophet famously declared that the differing viewpoints among the learned are a mercy from God. Whilst the literalist schools tend to be intolerant of others' interpretation, therefore, the opposite is the case as far as mainstream Muslim theology is concerned, whose scholars will usually not only insist on the literalist's right to his interpretation, but also argue that if the viewpoint is sincerely held then the literalist is obliged to follow it in preference to others' interpretations. Tolerance of, and respect for, difference is thus an important feature of mainstream Islam.

Muslims raised in Britain therefore live in a tolerant, liberal democracy and are part of a religion whose tolerance they often espouse. Yet it would seem to be the case that at least some young Muslims are attracted towards narrower interpretations of their religion that can constitute a danger – the 7/7 bombers, all from mainstream backgrounds, were evidently radicalized into such 'fundamentalist' views. I would like to turn to the clinical situation to explore the question of whether there is a relationship between this turn to fundamentalism and internalized racism. Does the fact of growing up under everyday Islamophobia play a part? How does the fact that 'Islamic fundamentalism', as I have argued, is inscribed within an internal racist defensive organization against terror affect the situation?

Ahmed

Some months after 9/11, Ahmed, as I shall call him, a man in his early 20s, had been driven to the verge of a breakdown by a fear that he would be arrested and handed over to the Americans. His anxiety stemmed from the fact that he had, in the 1990s, spent time in Afghanistan and Pakistan, and it was widely known that, in their determination to close in on the Al-Qā'idah network, the security services were now systematically tracing young men who had travelled there. No doubt he fitted their profile of potential suspects and it was surely only a matter of time before he would be rounded up. He could not eat or sleep, had lost several stone in weight and was only barely holding down his teaching job at a local mosque. His fear was such that he would not give me his real name, address or telephone number, and I could reach him only via a quite anonymous email address. In the consulting room, however, his panic responded to interpretation and he recovered his psychological mindedness with relative ease. For example, after some initial resistance he accepted an interpretation that he hated his father, and could see that the Russian forces, whose actions in Chechnya had so enraged him, stood for his Godless father. That must be why he had thought for some time that he needed psychological help, he said. Why had he not acted on this before going to Afghanistan?

Ahmed, the only son in a family of Pakistani origin, was the oldest of four children, all of them approximately two years apart. His father had immigrated to the UK in his teens, with his family, but he struggled with English and thus could not settle in school. He left as soon as he could – better to work and supplement the family income than endure the agony of displacement at school. In his mid-20s he had an arranged marriage to a distant relative in Pakistan. His wife joined him in the UK shortly after, and Ahmed was born about two years later, when his mother was approximately 21; by the time she was 30 she had had all four of her children.

Mrs A was a housewife who was naturally warm and got pleasure from raising her children. A devout Muslim, she taught them religious rites such as prayers, etc. and took an active interest in their schooling. His father, a hard-working taxi-driver largely absent from the family home was, in his eyes, not as observant a Muslim as his mother. In fact, he suspected that his father's work as a taxi-driver had brought him too close to the world of drink and drugs, easy women and prostitution; did he keep his distance or, when he was out late into the night, did he lead another secret, shadowy life? He thought he had, from time to time, overheard arguments between his parents that ran along these lines. On the surface, however, they were a happy family – part of a larger, close-knit extended family – whose children were popular and did well both at school and in the religious classes they attended in their local mosque afterwards.

At home they spoke Punjabi, but his mother began to learn English once he started nursery school as she was determined not to be left out of her children's education. Despite this attempt at involvement in their education, however, he felt that his parents really had no idea of the awful racist taunts and the ongoing prejudice they were subjected to in their working-class school. In fact, education was so highly prized that just about any complaint about school frustrated and annoyed their parents and thus fell on deaf ears. Nevertheless, all the children did well, and he himself obtained A-levels good enough to gain entry to university. However, he was uncertain as to what career to pursue – he had varied interests and strengths – hence his teachers suggested a gap year.

During the Bosnian War some years previously, he had become increasingly distressed by the fact that the international community, by failing to intervene to prevent the Bosnian genocide, appeared deaf to the plight of the Muslim. How could this happen in a Europe that was always at pains to remember the lessons of the Holocaust? To him this confirmed that today's Muslims were the Jews of the 1930s and 1940s, and he came to the view that if Muslims do not help one another, no one will. Now, whilst doing his A-levels, the war in Chechnya gathered pace, once again filling television screens with footage of cruel brutality towards European Muslims. Again the world seemed powerless or unwilling to act, but he drew comfort from reports that foreigners – 'Arabs' – were fighting alongside Chechen forces. Perhaps they too felt the way he did, and it was then that the idea of going to Afghanistan to train militarily took hold.

Once his exams were over, he told his parents he would spend a gap year in Pakistan – based with relatives but with the aim of travelling around – before deciding on his course of study. Once there he proceeded to the Afghan border, from where he found his way to camps where he was assimilated into the ranks of a training organization of sorts. However, whilst he anticipated a military machine in which he would be trained in the use of firearms to fight the Russian army in Chechnya, it turned out that they were being trained in bomb-making. It did not take long for him to realize that a campaign of terror against Western targets, in which innocent civilians would inevitably be caught up, was the goal. These were the very scenes in Chechnya that had so appalled him, and he returned to Pakistan, eventually finding his way to two Middle Eastern capitals where he enrolled in university courses in Arabic and Islamic Studies. He returned to the UK periodically until, two years previously, he was offered a teaching job in his local mosque.

By the end of the two assessment sessions it was clear that, under the terms within which George W. Bush's war on terror was being waged, there was a real risk of him being arrested, extradited and quite possibly ending up at Guantanamo Bay. At best he might be seen as a source of useful information on the enemy in Afghanistan; at worst as a member of a sleeper cell trained in bomb-making – from their point of view he would, of course, now be trying to minimize it – infiltrated back into the West awaiting further instructions. I thought his presenting anxiety was thus probably more realistic rather than primarily stemming from within. I offered to take him on for psychotherapy to investigate more fully the inner scenario underpinning his anxiety, to see how he might be helped. He agreed but in the event did not arrive. I heard no more from him and had no response to my two follow-up emails.

A Provisional Formulation

The events described by Ahmed are all from his adolescence, a period when the key developmental task is to find and take on an identity of one's own (Erikson 1968). A maturing intellect facilitates this engagement – abstract ideas can be toyed with, tried on for size, subjected to critical scrutiny, embraced with passion, opposing views dismissed, discarded, etc., all of which allow for the sublimation of altogether more powerful inner forces. This inner drama is directly related to changes in the body: greater anxiety and tension stems partly from a higher level of passion – libido – brought about by increased hormonal levels, but also from the fact that, with a maturing body, fantasies can be enacted in real time in a way that is not possible for the child – one can now rape, attack or murder a hated other. Fantasy is thus no longer as safe a container of unwanted and dangerous impulses as it was in childhood (Laufer & Laufer 1984).

Adolescents usually create temporary containers in the outside world for these forces. The peer group assumes special significance, with rival gangs, etc., giving voice to polarized positions, each adhered to with such passion that imagined battles, sometimes spilling over into the real world, are inevitable. Just by hanging out in gangs adolescents can terrorize adults, thereby successfully projecting their fear of the intensity of what is going on within. There are also usually attempts to bind destructive energies – smoking, alcohol, drugs and risk in general become particularly attractive. Causes, too, become important, with rigorous arguments developed to justify strong feelings for or against. Together, these channels promote the growth process in adolescence, and when they are unavailable it is that much harder for the adolescent to make the transition to an authentic role in the adult world – even if previous developmental stages were successfully negotiated – resulting in what Erikson termed role diffusion, a chronic inability to take up a stable, authentic identity of our own in the wider world.

In Ahmed's account one can see such normal adolescent processes at work. The father of his childhood, with whom he is destined to identify, is a dark and seedy sexual object – the result of projection into him of Ahmed's own split-off sexual and aggressive impulses deriving from his hatred of his father as an oedipal rival. With such a father he cannot identify – it would conflict with his religious nature, a living symbol within of his mother's love and care. He uses the panoply of adolescent manoeuvres to stage this conflict in the outside world – for example, the conflict between father and son is located in the civil war in Bosnia, the absence of an international community able to intervene expresses his intense anxiety that the murderousness between father and son is uncontainable – there is a genocide. Along the way, he is also working out a cause that he cares about, clarifying the principle that the innocent women and children, standing for his mother and sisters, should be protected. Unlike his father, he as a man will be there to do so. Once the inner situation has been projected into the world outside, movement is possible – he can join battle, knowing both his beliefs and also the risks that go with standing up for them. Having engaged in this, his own battle by the time he got to Afghanistan, it is no surprise that he recognized that his putative trainers' fight was not his, and thus had no stomach for it.

Further Exploration: The Islamist

Had Ahmed become my patient I would no doubt have learned in more detail how he used the outside world in order to play out what is usually a prolonged struggle involving these intense inner forces. For such an account we can turn to Ed Husain's (2007) book *The Islamist*, which describes in detail a journey through this same terrain (although it does not involve an attempt at military training). From a roughly comparable background – although Husain's father was actively involved with the community of believers and appears to have been more hands-on in the family – during his late teens and early 20s Husain too is pulled into what is now seen as the world of fundamentalist Islam. As leader of the Islamic Society at his college, he is drawn first to modernist political commentators whose analysis highlights the role of European colonialism in creating the abject conditions that prevail in Muslim countries, which neo-colonialist domination – in which corrupt ruling elites have a vested interest – maintains. The defeat of the Muslim empires of the past is seen as a crucial factor in this situation, and a return to Islamic rule becomes the explicit goal. He is inspired, at first, by writers who work, by democratic means, for a properly conceived Muslim state in the existing polities in the Indian subcontinent, then on to *Hizb-ut-Tahrir* [Party of Liberation], whose rallying cry is for the restoration, across the entire Muslim world, of the *khilafah* [caliphate], the system by which the Prophet and his immediate successors governed[5] and is therefore believed to be God-given. This will deliver us all. As it happens, his father, a follower of Sufi [spiritual] Islam, is a staunch opponent of such thinkers.

---

5. They view the Ottoman Empire as the last embodiment of this system.

Over the next few years Husain is increasingly drawn into the world of *Hizb-ut-Tahrir*. He neglects his studies, frequenting instead semi-secret study groups where the writings of the founder are studied and the group's take on global events is worked on, each analysis careful to 'spread the ideas'. What were these ideas? That democracy is an evil invention of the West, intended to subjugate and enslave, whereas in the golden age of Islam – when Europe was in the Dark Ages – things were altogether better. All must therefore unite and work for the messianic coming of the *khaleefah* – the undisputed leader of the faithful – who will govern justly and in the benign way that characterized the Prophet's rule in Medina. How? By opposing the system of the unbelieving West at every opportunity, arguing for the superiority of Islam, and enlisting the masses. This is seen as superior to the empty ritual prayers of ordinary Muslims, like his parents. He becomes an activist, spreading the ideas at every opportunity with the aim of making a public impact. Doing so passes for taking on leadership of the community, just as hurling intellectual bullet points strategically at opponents passes as being a master of debate. He believed, encouraged by hints from those higher up and supposedly in the know, that they were part of a global network in which something big was about to happen. For instance, 'brothers' in the armed forces of Muslim countries (especially where party members were in prison) would take power and install the *khaleefah*, and we in the West must be ready to join in. Once in place it was the global Muslim Army, at this very moment being secretly assembled – had he himself not been secretly recruited? – from within the armed forces of Middle Eastern countries that would fight to protect the Muslims of Bosnia, Chechnya, Palestine, etc.

Within the microcosm of the London student world, therefore, Husain was caught up in a semi-secret gang, which allowed him to live out a sophisticated rebellion against his father, as he himself now recognizes. This was played out on a larger public stage – first against the authorities at the College, who are completely defeated, then in a wider rhetorical crusade against the infidel West. Eventually the battle runs its course when he recognizes the Stalinist way in which the leadership really operates, which lacks the self-reflection and integrity associated with sincere attempts to follow Islamic scripture. This recognition emerges also as a result of a knifing in which the assailant, a martial arts expert who had previously been encouraged to see himself as a defender of his brothers and sisters, is completely disowned and left to face the music as an individual, a stance that is devoid of genuine compassion for one's fellows. Finally, he returns to his father's brand of Islam but in a new way.

In the psychological function that it performs for him, Husain's fundamentalist organization is, I think, indistinguishable from organizations such as the Communist Party, whose global aspiration in the name of a noble cause can so attract and inspire youth. We recognize that these play a vital role in society. In its secrecy it also resembles adolescent gangs whose violent opposition to authority can be expressed through the use of drugs, etc., and is sometimes accompanied by a shared notion of how much the previous generation has messed things up. In this reading, therefore, one could say that both Husain and Ahmed were lucky to live in a tolerant society in which they had an avenue available to work through their adolescent conflict and find a more or less satisfactory role within their world. This suggests that the 'fundamentalist' voice in our society is a valuable one, paradoxically preventing these two from being recruited into the arms of terrorists by providing a vehicle for living out, and hence containing, their inner adolescent conflict.

The Effect of Racism

This reading sees both Ahmed's and Husain's difficulties as part of the normal developmental work of adolescence. However, there is a further matter I would like to return to, namely the fact that they are both members of a minority out-group subjected to the forces of everyday racism. Ahmed felt that eagerness for their children to obtain an education made his parents deaf to their ongoing experience of racial harassment and abuse at school. If we bear in mind that the us–them divisions in our contemporary world continue to bear the mark of colonialism (Treacher 2005), we have a broader context within which to consider the significance of this factor. The legacy of growing up in a divided colonial world, Frantz Fanon (1952) argues, is that the 'black' person develops a dual self (Davids 1996) – here, a white English one and a Muslim Pakistani one. As a result of the imbalance in power and prestige between these two positions in the outside world, the white self is inevitably idealized and the Pakistani/Muslim one denigrated. He went on to suggest that the process by which this alienating identification is inscribed in the mind is a violent one:

> It is obvious that the agents of government [i.e. policeman, soldier] speak the language of pure force [in enforcing oppression]. The intermediary [i.e. teacher, social worker, law officer] does not lighten the oppression, nor seek to hide the domination; he shows them up and puts them into practice with the clear conscience of an upholder of the peace; yet he is the bringer of violence into the home and *into the mind* of the native. (Fanon 1967, p. 28, my italics)

In their adolescence, both Husain and Ahmed took ownership of this problem by explicitly taking on a particular, magnified version of their unconsciously denigrated Muslim identities. At this stage, a deep split was in operation and aspects of the self associated with being Western were projected into the Westerner/unbeliever, allowing the process of engagement between the two to begin. What Ahmed's parents could not hear, therefore, he himself made room for in his adolescence; following Fanon, I am suggesting that the violent hatred characterizing the relationship in the mind between Muslim (e.g. Chechen) and non-Muslim (e.g. Russian) can be accounted for by the violence against the Muslim self attending the process by which the white/Western identification was inscribed in the mind (Davids 1996). This is the inevitable psychic consequence of growing up as a member of a disadvantaged, disempowered group.

The Reluctant Fundamentalist

What happens when, in adolescence, the opportunity to take personal responsibility for the internal split is evaded? I can explore this through Mohsin Hamid's (2007) novel, *The Reluctant Fundamentalist*, where Changez, the narrator, exemplifies the problem. An extremely bright and gifted young Pakistani from a Lahore aristocratic family now in somewhat reduced circumstances, he is sent to New York where he excels. After graduating from Princeton he is appointed to a prestigious and highly competitive consultancy where he soon proves to be their top new recruit. Although he flourishes in the New York meritocracy:

> There were moments when I became disorientated ... [On an assignment in the Philippines] I was riding with my colleagues in a limousine. We were mired in traffic, unable to move, and I glanced out the window to see, only a few feet away, the driver of a jeepney returning my gaze. There was an undisguised hostility in his expression; I had no idea why. We had not met before ... But his dislike was so obvious, so *intimate*, that it got under my skin ...
>
> Afterwards, I tried to understand why he acted as he did. Perhaps, I thought, his wife has just left him; perhaps he simply does not like Americans. I remained preoccupied with this matter longer than I should have, pursuing several possibilities that all assumed – as their unconscious starting point – that he and I shared a sort of Third World sensibility. Then one of my colleagues asked me a question, and when I turned to answer him something rather strange took place. I looked at him – at his fair hair and light eyes and, most of all, at his oblivious immersion in the minutiae of our work – and thought, you are so *foreign*. I felt at that moment much closer to the Filipino driver than to him; I felt I was play-acting when in reality I ought to be making my way home ... (Hamid 2007, pp. 76–7)

However, this remains merely a discordant note: 'I was the only non-American in our group, but I suspected my Pakistaniness was invisible, cloaked by my suit, by my expense account, and – most of all – by my companions' (p. 82).

Such discordant notes were, of course, the very ones that Husain and Ahmed had heeded, embarking on a journey to reclaim their Muslim self and turning against the white Western self in the process. This brought them considerable trouble. Changez takes the opposite course, turns a deaf ear to them and proceeds, instead, to intensify his Western identification. He falls in love with the intelligent, gifted and beautiful but fragile Erica, a fellow Princeton graduate. She, in turn, seems to warm to him but something holds her back. It turns out that she is completely taken up with her true love, her childhood soul-mate who had tragically died. After one abortive attempt at lovemaking, Changez encourages her to pretend that he is her departed lover, an act of selfless sacrifice on his part that succeeds in igniting real passion in her. However, it leaves Changez insatiably hungry, a portent to the unravelling of the life he had made in New York.

We can see the successful intercourse as confronting him forcefully with the recognition that, in order to be loved, he has had to become someone else. Now, in the intimacy of the sexual union with Erica, he is confronted by the alienation that stands at his core; the discordant notes that have been tugging at his consciousness, signifying an identity that has been repressed, can no longer be ignored. In the post-9/11 era the strategy of sacrificing his Pakistani/Muslim identity has already been undermined as he is repeatedly reminded, painfully, that he is one of 'them'. On his way back from the Philippines he is separated off from his colleagues and detained at the airport, and in a parking lot the racist taunt, 'Arab', turns him murderous. The successful intercourse is the final straw that confronts him with this 'otherness' within and gradually brings on a catastrophic breakdown, ushering in a descent into a 'fundamentalist' mindset whose sense of danger hovers throughout. Gradually he destroys the very success he has built and returns to Pakistan, becoming, we assume, the reluctant fundamentalist of the title. What this entails, however, remains unclear, and the prospect of a violent return of the repressed hangs suspended over the novel from beginning to end.

It was Frantz Fanon (1967) who first argued that violent resistance (rather than passive submission) was both the path to political emancipation *and also* a prerequisite for the mental health of the oppressed since it held out the promise of undoing the internal racist denigration of the black self (Dalal 2002; Davids 1996). In my reading, in all three instances – Ahmed, Husain and Changez – the existence of a fundamentalist voice facilitated the journey towards a more integrated identity. The first two, citizens from birth of a society that tolerated a fundamentalist voice within, provided a vehicle that facilitated this transition without a catastrophic breakdown of the personality. Changez was not so lucky.

References

Ahmed, K. (2002) The Exeter experience. In: *Quest for Sanity: Reflections on September 11 and the Aftermath*, pp. 188–91. London: Muslim Council of Britain.
Allen, C. (2002) Islamophobia in the EU post-September 11. In: *Quest for Sanity: Reflections on September 11 and the Aftermath*, pp. 136–43. London: Muslim Council of Britain.
Allen, C. & Nielsen, J.S. (2002) *Summary Report on Islamophobia in the EU after 11 September 2001*. Vienna: European Monitoring Centre on Racism and Xenophobia.

Blank, D.R. (1999) A veil of controversy: The construction of a 'Tchador Affair' in the French press. *Interventions: International Journal of Postcolonial Studies* 1(4): 536–54.

Bunglawala, I. (2002). British Muslims and the media. In: *Quest for Sanity: Reflections on September 11 and the Aftermath*, pp. 43–52. London: Muslim Council of Britain.

Bunglawala, I. (2004). Review of *Islamophobia: Issues, Challenges and Action*, ed. R. Richardson. Report of the Commission on British Muslims and Islamophobia [Electronic Version], 20 October 2004. Available from: http://www.mcb.org.uk/library/Inayat-Islamophobia.pdf/

Dalal, F. (2002) *Race, Colour and the Processes of Racialization: New Perspectives from Psychoanalysis, Group Analysis and Sociology*. Hove, New York, NY: Brunner-Routledge.

Davids, M.F. (1996) Frantz Fanon: The struggle for inner freedom. *Free Associations* 6(2): 205–34.

Davids, M.F. (2003) The internal racist. *Bulletin of the British Psychoanalytical Society* 39(4): 1–15.

Erikson, E.H. (1968) *Identity: Youth and Crisis*. London: Faber and Faber.

Fanon, F. (1952) *Black Skin, White Masks*, trans. C.L. Markmann. London: Pluto Press, 1986.

Fanon, F. (1967) *The Wretched of the Earth*, trans. C. Farrington. Harmondsworth: Penguin.

Freud, S. (1922) Some neurotic mechanisms in jealousy, paranoia and homosexuality. *SE* 18, pp. 221–32. London: Hogarth.

Hamid, M. (2007) *The Reluctant Fundamentalist*. London, New York, NY: Penguin Books.

Husain, E. (2007) *The Islamist*. London, New York, NY: Penguin Books.

Laufer, M. & Laufer, M.E. (1984) *Adolescence and Developmental Breakdown: A Psychoanalytic View*. New Haven, CT: Yale University Press.

MCB (2002) *Quest for Sanity: Reflections on September 11 and the Aftermath*. London: Muslim Council of Britain.

RunnymedeTrust (1997) *Islamophobia: A Challenge for Us All*. London: The Runnymede Trust.

Said, E. (1997) *Covering Islam*. New York, NY: Vintage.

Seabrook, J. (2004) Religion as a fig leaf for racism: The BNP is now riding a broader wave of respectable Islamophobia. *The Guardian*, 23 July.

Segal, H. (2003) The mind of the fundamentalist/terrorist: Not learning from experience – Hiroshima, the Gulf War and 11 September. *News and Events Annual Issue*. Available from: http://www.psychoanalysis.org.uk/

Sheridan, L. (2002) Religious discrimination: The new racism. In: *Quest for Sanity: Reflections on September 11 and the Aftermath*, pp. 86–93. London: Muslim Council of Britain.

Steiner, J. (1987) The interplay between pathological organisations and the paranoid–schizoid and depressive positions. *International Journal of Psychoanalysis* 68: 69–80.

Stuttaford, A. (2004) Veil of tears: Absurdity in France [21 April]. Retrieved 21 October 2004. Available from: http://www.nationalreview.com/stuttaford/stuttaford200404210855.asp/

Summers, F. (2006) Fundamentalism, psychoanalysis, and psychoanalytic theories. *Psychoanalytic Review* 93: 329–52.

Treacher, A. (2005) On postcolonial subjectivity. *Group Analysis* 38(1): 43–57.

Whitaker, B. (2002) Islam and the British press. In: *Quest for Sanity: Reflections on September 11 and the Aftermath*, pp. 53–7. London: Muslim Council of Britain.

ABSTRACT

Muslims, as members of minority communities in the West, grow up against a background of everyday Islamophobia. I suggest that the Muslim self internalized in such a setting is denigrated (Fanon 1952), a problem usually grappled with during adolescence when identity formation is the key developmental task. This typically involves the adolescent taking on polarized positions and embracing extreme causes. Following the 9/11 and 7/7 attacks Islamophobia intensified, which can be understood, at the psychological level, as an internal racist defence against overwhelming anxiety. Within that defensive organization, which I describe, fundamentalism is inscribed as the problematic heart of Islam, complicating the adolescent's attempt to come to terms with the inner legacy of everyday Islamophobia. I explore these themes through a case study of a young man who travelled to Afghanistan in the 1990s, and by brief reference to Ed Husain's *The Islamist* and Mohsin Hamid's novel *The Reluctant Fundamentalist*.

Key words: fundamentalism, Islamophobia, adolescence, identity, internal racism

DOI: 10.3366/E1460823509000397

PSYCHOANALYSIS, ISLAM, AND THE OTHER
OF LIBERALISM[1]

Joseph Massad, New York, USA

One of the difficulties in analysing what Islam has come to *mean* and to refer to since the 19th century is the absence of agreement on what Islam actually *is*. Does *Islam* name a religion, a geographical site, a communal identity; is it a concept, a technical term, a sign, or a taxonomy? The lack of clarity on whether it could be all these things at the same time is compounded by the fact that Islam has acquired referents and significations it did not formerly possess. European Orientalists and Muslim and Arab thinkers begin to use 'Islam' in numerous ways while seemingly convinced that it possesses an immediate intelligibility that requires no specification or definition. 'Islam', for these thinkers, is not only the *name* the Qur'an attributes to the *din* (often (mis)translated as religion, though there is some disagreement about this) that entails a faith [*iman*] in God disseminated by the Prophet Muhammad, but can also refer to the history of Muslim states and empires, the different bodies of philosophical, theological, jurisprudential, medical, literary, and scientific works, as well as to culinary, sexual, social, economic, religious, ritualistic, scholarly, agricultural, and urban practices engaged in by Muslims from the 7th to the 19th century and beyond, and much, much more. What kinds of modernist projects, intellectual endeavours and critiques, types of politics, forms of political life, spirituality, and economic and cultural practices do the new meanings and referents of Islam enable and what kinds do they disable?

Some of the new meanings and referents of Islam had a significant impact on political and social thought as well as on national and international politics in the 19th and 20th centuries and may have even more of an impact

---

1. This paper is a shorter version of an essay commissioned for a Special Issue on 'Islam' of the journal *Umbr(a)*, edited by Joan Copjec, to appear in June/July 2009.

JOSEPH MASSAD is Associate Professor of Modern Arab Politics and Intellectual History. He is author of *Colonial Effects: The Making of National Identity in Jordan* (New York, NY: Columbia University Press, 2001), *The Persistence of the Palestinian Question: Essays on Zionism and the Palestinians* (London: Routledge, 2006), and *Desiring Arabs* (Chicago, IL: University of Chicago Press, 2007). Address for correspondence: MEALAC, Columbia University, 614 Kent Hall, New York, NY 10027, USA. [jam25@columbia.edu]

in the 21st. The implication of these meanings on politics and society results from their transformation of Islam into a 'culture' and a 'civilization' or a 'cultural tradition' (Von Grunebaum 1955), a 'system' (Margoliouth 1896), a *'manhaj'* [way of life, method] (Qutb 2005; Shakir 1992),[2] a 'programme' (Asad 1947, pp. 5, 14, 152), an ethics, a code of public conduct, a gendered sartorial code, banking principles, a type of governance. Moreover, 'Islam' has also come to be deployed as a metonym: *fiqh* [problematically rendered jurisprudence] and *kalam* [theology, again, problematically], traditionally sciences established by Muslim thinkers, or *Shari'ah* ['sacred law', also problematically], a term loaded with different connotations and trajectories, often referring to a body of opinions and interpretations, come to be conceived as constituent parts of 'Islam', for which it can metonym-ically substitute.[3]

While the easiest transformation to identify is the one that makes Islam over into a 'culture' and a 'civilization', given the centrality of this meaning among Orientalist thinkers and their Muslim and Arab counterparts since the 19th century, the production of Islam's many other new meanings and referents may not be as clear. Yet a history of the multiplication of the meanings of Islam is necessary for understanding what Islam has become in today's world, both in those parts of the world where peoples, political and social forces claim to uphold one kind of Islam or another and in those parts of the world where peoples, political and social forces see 'Islam' as 'other', whether or not they 'oppose' it. Indeed, the current ongoing war is itself not only part of the productive process of endowing Islam with new meanings and referents, but also of the related process of controlling the slippage of the term towards specific and particular meanings and referents and away from others. In this way 'Islam' is being opposed to certain antonyms ('the West', 'liberalism', 'individualism', 'democracy', or 'freedom') and decidedly not to others ('oppression', 'dictatorship', or 'injustice').

Two central religious and intellectual strands emerged in the 19th century among Arab, Muslim, and European Orientalist thinkers who argued for the compatibility or incompatibility of 'Islam' with Western modernity and progress. The word or, more precisely, name 'Islam' itself began to conjure up immediate comprehension and significance in ways assumed to have always been the case. This project of rethinking (about) 'Islam' in new ways, while often passing itself off as a return to old or original ways of thinking, was situated in the political context of the rise of

---

2. Sayyid Qutb uses the term 'manhaj' throughout his writings, especially in *Al-Islam wa Mushkilat al-Hadarah* [Islam and the Problems of Civilization] (Cairo: Dar al-Shuruq, 2005), as does Mahmud Muhammd Shakir in his *Risalah fi al-Tariq ila Thaqafatina* [A Letter on the Path to Our Culture] (Cairo: Mu'assasat al-Risalah, 1992).

3. Dale F. Eickelman and James Piscatori have written perceptively about the 'systematization' of Islam and its 'objectification' and how the latter 'reconfigures the symbolic production of Muslim politics'. For them, however, Islam denotes a 'religion' and not multiple referents (Eickelman & Piscatori 1996, p. 38).

European imperial thought and territorial expansion and the corresponding decline of Ottoman political and imperial power. Yet the 'Islam' to which these European and non-European thinkers referred was a more expansive concept encompassing phenomena that had hitherto been seen as extraneous to it. Indeed, 'Islam' had never been the catch-all term the 19th century would make of it, but was, rather, something more specific, more particular.

Another of the more interesting aspects of post-19th century uses of the term, 'Islam', is not just its accretion of referents, but also that the accreted meanings were deployed not only by different thinkers or different intellectual or political trends, but especially by each thinker and each trend. European Orientalists, Arab secularists (Muslim and Christian), pious (and later Islamist) thinkers, post-colonial states, defining themselves as 'Muslim' or 'Islamic' and their 'Western' and 'secular' opponents, all seem to use the term 'Islam' in a variety of ways to refer to a whole range of things. The productive multiplication of referents that Islam would begin to acquire would ultimately destabilize whatever meaning it had had before or even *after* this transformation, in that it is not always clear in modern writing about Islam which referent it has in a given text. Rather, it often seems that all of them are in play interchangeably *in the same text* as well as across texts, thus rendering 'Islam' a catachresis that always stands in for the *wrong* referent.

Psychoanalysts and psychoanalytic thinkers working more recently on the object called 'Islam' have been active participants in this process of multiplying significations, referents, and antonyms with little self-questioning or analysis of what they are doing. Historically, psychoanalysis did not take 'Islam' as an object of study or as a concern or problem. Except for Freud's passing comments in *Moses and Monotheism* about 'the founding of the Mohammedan religion' seeming to be 'an abbreviated repetition of the Jewish one, of which it emerged as an imitation' (Freud 1939, p. 91), little was written on the topic. Indeed, psychoanalytic studies on religion have been remarkable for the absence of any mention of Islam. This includes, for example, the early study by Erich Fromm (1950) on the topic, which makes no mention at all of Islam, while attending to Christianity, Judaism, 'Buddhism', and 'Hinduism'.

Arab psychoanalytic thinkers, including Moustapha Safouan, Fethi Benslama, Adnan Hoballah, and Georges Tarabishi, who are without exception male and located in France and whose studies focus on psychoanalysis and Islam (except for Tarabishi who is the only one writing in Arabic and who writes on Arab intellectuals and Arabic literature),[4] started to write on the linkage between the two in the context of the rise of

---

4. Tarabishi, more recently, started to write on 'Islam', and occasionally punctuates his texts with psychoanalytic references, as he does in *Hartaqat 2: 'an al-'Ilmaniyyah ka-Ishkaliyyah Islamiyyah-Islamiyyah* (Tarabishi 2008).

Islamisms, which have acted as a trigger for their interventions.[5] In a longer study, I attempt to trace their perception of Islamisms as a 'return of the repressed', namely, Islam, when it should have disappeared a long time ago. This 'return' reopens the scene of the trauma of the persistence of Islam as 'religion' in the life of Arabs and Muslims, which causes our psychoanalysts embarrassment and 'shame' before their European counterparts and, more importantly, before their Europeanized selves. Indeed, much of their writing on this question uncovers a deep narcissistic injury that, as Arabs and Muslims, as Europeanized Arabs and Muslims who grew up in modernizing times that sought Europeanization as the telos of modernity to which all Arabs and Muslims were supposedly headed, they now inhabit times wherein the project of Europeanization had failed as a result of the 'return' of Islam in the form of Islamisms. Due to time limitations, I will focus my remarks on the work of Tunisian psychoanalyst Fethi Benslama in an attempt to examine the intellectual and psychic mechanisms at work in his thinking on this interesting but uninterrogated conjunction of a reified psychoanalysis and a reified Islam.

Benslama's (2002) *La psychanalyse à l'épreuve de l'Islam* is perhaps the most serious engagement with one possible relationship that a certain psychoanalysis could have with a certain 'Islam', namely one in which this psychoanalysis is put (or puts itself?) to the test of this 'Islam'. Benslama thinks he is, or wishes he were, writing a corollary to Freud's *Moses and Monotheism*, along the lines of 'Muhammad and Monotheism'. This is in fact his second attempt to do so. His first book *La nuit brisée* [The Shattered Night], published in 1988, was less explicitly presented as such a project. *La psychanalyse à l'épreuve de l'Islam* is a more profound second attempt, a *repetition*, at an engagement with that very same project, and intensifies Benslama's dependence on *Moses and Monotheism* as the main psychoanalytic and Freudian scripture that guides him.

One of the more brilliant achievements of Benslama's book is his exploration of the role of Abraham and Ishmael as the father and grandfather of the Arabs and of the fact that the Qur'an, following the Torah, imposed the figure of non-Arab Ishmael (whose mother is the Egyptian Hagar and father the Hebrew Abraham) on Arab lineage which was never resisted by the post-Islamic Arabs, even though neither Abraham nor Ishmael had any presence in their cosmological lore prior to the

---

5. Indeed, Benslama recognizes this clearly, by excepting himself as having shown interest in 'Islam' earlier than his colleagues. He states that his initial interest in 'Islam' had started due to an encounter with Pierre Fedida after which he published his first book dealing with psychoanalysis and Islam in 1988 'when Islam had not constituted yet a sharp problem in the international public sphere, nor a question for psychoanalytic research' (Benslama 2004a, p. 77). For Benslama's first book on the subject, see Benslama 1988. This is an interesting assertion since the more usual dating of the international interest in 'Islam' coincides with the Iranian Revolution of 1978/1979.

Qur'anic moment. (Here, Benslama seems to ignore the fact that in contrast to pagan Arab tribes, for Jewish Arab tribes, perhaps not considered Arabs by him, Ishmael and Abraham were indeed present.) Unlike Freud's Moses, who is exposed contra the Jewish scriptural and theological tradition as an Egyptian outsider to his chosen people, Benslama's Ishmael, who is not the main prophet of the Muhammadan call, is not revealed to be non-Arab, as this is not a hidden part of his lineage in the Qur'an and in Islamic theology. But rather what Benslama aims to do is to discuss his non-Arabness in relation to the question of identity and maternalism, the way Hagar is repressed in Islamic theology and Arab identity-formations in favour of Sarah, without much deviation from the Judaic story. To some extent, Benslama's discussion corresponds to Edward Said's important reading of Freud's *Moses and Monotheism* as an anti-nationalist call that rejects essentialism and group homogeneity as necessary founding myths. Said concludes his discussion of Freud's *Moses*:

> In other words, identity cannot be thought or worked through itself alone; it cannot constitute or even imagine itself without that radical originary break or flaw which will not be repressed, because Moses was Egyptian, and therefore always outside the identity inside which so many have stood and suffered – and later, perhaps, even triumphed. (Said 2003, p. 54)

Benslama in contrast wants to read the repression of Hagar as informing 'Islam's' views of women and the figure of the mother more generally: 'Islam was born from the stranger at the origins of monotheism, and this stranger remained a stranger in Islam' (Benslama 2002, p. 171).

Benslama however does not limit himself to a discussion of paternity and maternity and the question of origins in the Qur'an and subsequent theological exegesis, but wants to bring his conclusions to bear on the contemporary situation. It is made obvious throughout the text that the entire archaeological project that Benslama is engaged in is precisely aimed at responding to the claims put forth by many contemporary Islamisms and their enemies concerning Islam and Islamic origins. It is in this context that Benslama's book shows less engagement with psychoanalytic readings and shifts to liberal critiques.

Definitionally, Benslama is aware that 'Islam' is multiple and that it is always already 'Islams'. Yet at key moments in his narrative these multiple 'Islams' slip into a singular one which is conflated with a singular 'Islamism' both as an utterable name and as one that should only be used under erasure ['*sous rature*']. My concern has to do with the ideological context of these slippages, as conscious and unconscious, to better understand the political philosophy and psychic processes that inform them. While he does not define Islam in his book, Benslama provides two meanings in a later article on the subject, namely that the word 'Islam' 'has been fixed by a theological connotation into "an abandonment to God" ["*un abandon à Dieu*"]' and that its etymology designates this act as 'having been saved after being abandoned' (Benslama 2004a, p. 79). The latter in fact may be one of the possible connotations of the word but not necessarily its immediate one, as the most common meaning of Islam in Arabic is 'deliverance [of one's self] to God', and not 'abandonment', or the more common Orientalist translation of 'submission to God' which Benslama problematically cites as the 'theological' meaning of the word in Islam, even while offering its other meaning(s) of 'being saved', but, curiously, not its meaning of 'deliverance' (Benslama 1988, p. 176). Benslama is certainly not alone in his problematic translations. The problem of translation and of language is essential for psychoanalytic thinkers more generally. Moustapha Safouan posits his major thesis about what he constantly refers to as Arab 'backwardness' as a problem of language and, like Benslama, but with less erudition, often seems to confound Arabic and Latin etymologies in ways that exoticize modern Arabic, as he does, for example, in his discussion of the difference between the Latin-based word sovereignty and its Arabic equivalent *Siyadah* (Safouan 2007, p. 65). But I digress.

It is clear that the two meanings of Islam that Benslama posits are not the only possible referents of the term as Benslama uses it in *La psychanalyse à l'épreuve de l'Islam*. While at the outset Benslama explains that the many 'Islams' he posited are diverse and various, that they are sometimes unconnected, even though they may all be hiding 'behind' the singular name 'Islam' (Benslama 2002, p. 23), he would soon abandon this multiplicity in the interest of a singular Islam whose signified and referents in his use will remain multiple but unspecified while presented consciously and ideologically as singular. It is rarely made clear, for example, when he uses the term Islam, whether he is referring to all Islamist movements and individuals or just some of them, or if 'Islam' refers to the history of Islamic theology from the 7th century to the present, or if it refers to the history or present of states that call themselves Islamist or even those that call themselves 'Muslim', or if it is referring to the Qur'an, the Hadith, the Sunnah, or all combined, and so on and so forth. While Benslama sees the attempt to homogenize Islams into Islam as not only an Islamist project but also as a European 'superficial' attempt to deal with the rise of many 'Islamist' movements in different geographical and social contexts, their reduction by a European political sociology to one Islam, Benslama declares, is nothing short of 'resistance to the intelligibility of Islam' on the part of Islamologists, a resistance that, he maintains, also applies to European psychoanalysts (Benslama 2002, p. 24). This astute understanding of the multiplicity of Islams as signifiers, whose signifieds, however, remain obscure in Benslama's own text, falls by the wayside through his constant invoking of 'Islam' in the singular as a subject with a self that expresses itself and whose meaning is readily intelligible. Benslama speaks of the 'actuality of Islam' (Benslama 2002, p. 26) that imposes itself on him, of 'the tradition of Islam' (ibid., p. 27) within which people grow up, and how he had 'noted simply that, in the majority of cases [he consulted], Islam was always the effect and the cause of subjective and trans-individual structures' (ibid.).

In these telling slippages (and there are many more), what is most interesting is the commonality of the perception of the singularity of Islam and its effect on Muslims that Benslama shares with many of the Islamist thinkers themselves. Indeed, and in line with how many Islamists and Muslims reacted to Salman Rushdie's *The Satanic Verses*, Benslama identifies their reaction as occurring within the singular world of Islam. He states that the 'shock in the case of Islam came from whence we did not expect, from literary fiction that put on stage the truth of origins as a trick' (Benslama 2002, p. 43). In doing so, Benslama is following in a liberal secular tradition, which often seems to recognize the same Islam of some Islamists as the one 'Islam', even though he is well aware (and curiously adds a footnote to the Arabic edition of his book clarifying) that what is at stake [*enjeu*] in contemporary debates is the 'meaning of Islam', and what is unfolding is indeed 'a war of the name', or a nominalist war.[6] In his book, however, and despite his noted vigilance, Benslama opts not only to analyse the terms of this war but, and therein lies the contradiction, also to join in as a party to the war. In this light, the battle over the Islamist notion of Islam (which Benslama and many secularists often oppose as the one Islam), as many Islamists correctly claim, is between those who want to uphold 'Islam' and those who do not. In fact, he ambivalently posits this singular 'Islam', whose meaning he often shares with the Islamists and the Orientalists, as the other (or is it the Other?) of liberalism (Benslama 2002, p. 45).[7] He does not do so explicitly, but his invocation of 'freedom', 'tolerance', and 'individualism' as the values or key ingredients that are absent from the one Islam, and as the ingredients that would be included in the Islam he wishes for, structures his polemic against the Islamists. Moreover, his insistence that Islam be transformed from a *din* into the Christian and liberal notion 'religion' ['*La religion musulmane*'] (ibid., p. 24) and his attack on the Islamists who, unlike him and liberal common sense, regard 'Islam not only as a religion' (ibid., p. 25) commit him to a liberal epistemology whose aim is the assimilation of the world in its own image.

But there is an important ambivalence in Benslama's project. While this Islam seems according to him to be opposed to individual freedoms like those of writers of the calibre of Rushdie, he also criticizes European Islamologists for not recognizing that another Islam (whose referents again

6. Fathi Bin Salamah, *Al-Islam wa al-Tahlil al-Nafsi* (2008, p. 36 n.).

7. See *La psychanalyse à l'épreuve de l'Islam* (2002, p. 45) for Benslama's liberal defence of personal freedom and the individual.

remain multiple – the Qur'an, Islamic theology, Islamic 'culture', etc.) does uphold individualism. Benslama insists that:

> Islam rather deploys one of the extremely powerful dimensions of individuality, a dimension of great conceptual abundance. This dimension could not have developed without being compatible with the reality of the culture. This is indeed a culture of individuality, but one that is essentially governed by an identification with God. (Benslama 2002, p. 302)

Indeed, Benslama is very critical of Western psychoanalytical pronounce-ments on Islam and Muslim cultures as obliterating of the individual, and which see Western achievement that gave birth to the individual as the ultimate achievement of civilization *tout court*. He declares that these approaches that want to insist that the alleged absence of individualism in Islam prevents Muslims from being accessible to psychoanalysis are 'ignorant': 'I will not cite anyone's name so as not to privilege those who are in the order of ignorance and carelessness' (ibid.).

Benslama's ambivalence here is not necessarily and only a conscious ambivalence but more likely the effect of an ideological commitment, one that imagines different audiences differently. The reference to multiple Islams might be said to be the ideological position (the position of political correctness?) and/or an expression of a wish, while the reference to one singular Islam in the many slips could betray what Benslama actually *fears* to be the case. This could indicate his own unconscious resistance to the claim (his own claim) that there are many Islams, or his conscious recognition that his claim is a mere wish and not an acknowledgement of observable reality, and that what he does notice or 'realize', as he tells us, is that there actually exists only one Islam and therefore that this Islam must be opposed (hated?) for not pluralizing itself as it must and should. In this regard, he announces at the outset of the book that the origins of his own interest in writing on Islam as an intellectual task – which emerged in the early 1980s (elsewhere he would tell us that his interest started in the mid-1980s) (Benslama 2004a, p. 77) 'in a critical historical situation marked by a fanatical surge' – were to engage decidedly in the kind of thinking that explores 'the gap between a terminable Islam and an interminable one' (Benslama 2002, p. 20). While Benslama cautions us (and perhaps himself) to use a new vocabulary and to adjust to a new epistemology wherein we (he) must 'hear Islams when we say Islam', it would seem that he often remains deaf to his own cautionary warning (ibid., p. 76). Perhaps, then, the singularity of actual Islam is itself the scene of the trauma that one cannot but revisit and whose claims, one, or Benslama, is compelled to repeat at the very same moment and in the very same text where he insists that he and we must resist.

Indeed, *La psychanalyse à l'épreuve de l'Islam* repeats many of the scenes (and discussions) in the biography of the Prophet Muhammad that Benslama conjured up in *La nuit brisée*. It remains unclear if this act of repetition is merely a self-repetition that revisits his first (inaugural?) text (child?) on 'Islam' or a revisiting of the Prophetic scenes themselves as the site of trauma that compels repetition. *La psychanalyse à l'épreuve de l'Islam* surely is a repetition with a twist. It is a more comprehensive, more elaborated second attempt at producing a psychoanalytic reading of 'Islam'. As Benslama's youngest child on Islam (and, as we know, books which carry the names of their authors are always reproductively connected to them, just as children carry the name of the father), *La psychanalyse à l'épreuve de l'Islam* seems more privileged and more celebrated by critics, just like the younger male child in the Torah is always more privileged – Abel, Isaac, Jacob, and others. It is unclear if an unconscious wish on the part of Benslama is at work here, one of preferring, once again as God and Abraham did, Isaac to Ishmael.

Before I indulge in further speculations, let me cite Benslama's own statement of his task in his important book:

> to translate the Islamic origin into the language of Freudian deconstruction … Translation is not application or annexation, but through a signifying displacement, conveys the very texture of a tradition in its language and its images, in order to give access to what is unknowingly thought, inside it [*à son insu*]. (2002, p. 319)

I am unpersuaded by this assertion, mostly because often translation of 'Islamic' texts into European languages seems to mean retrieval of dictionary meanings of words and their etymology without much attention to the intellectual context and historicity of the uses and significations of words and how they change over time – the 'links' that Muhammad Arkun has juxtaposed as 'language–history–thought' (Arkun 1998, p. 16) – something all contemporary interpretative exercises of the texts of the past must attend to in order to avoid projecting contemporary meanings and values onto them. It is clear that Benslama is concerned that translation can be a form of annexation. But he wants to insist that translation in this case opens up an access to the unconscious of the tradition ['*à son insu*']. While this may be so, it does not do away with his initial concern. I would call translation in this case not 'annexation' but assimilation, in that, whether Benslama's 'Freudian deconstruction' uncovers an Islam that is individualist or anti-individualist, it could only uncover it in relation to a modern liberal European value that he posits as universal, namely 'individualism'. This assimilationist move is presented as useful for psychoanalysis and as useful psychoanalytically to the extent to which it allows 'the intelligibility of the logic of repression, which subtends the foundation of a symbolic organization' (Benslama 2002). There is some tension in this assimilationist project, however. On occasion, like the Orientalists, Benslama insists on *not* translating the Arabic word for God, 'Allah', into its French equivalent ['*Dieu*'] when translating an Islamist text from Arabic, but seems invested in exoticizing it as the specific and proper name of the Muslim God, when

in fact it is the name that Arab Christians had used for their God before
Muhammad and still use it after him (ibid., p. 59). Ultimately, however,
Benslama wants to present Islam as assimilable to the liberal notion of
the individual even if it is so with a difference. It is possible here that
Benslama is engaged in deploying this Islamic individualism as a way of
passing Islam off as European, and that this passing off is indeed a form
of resistance on his part to Orientalist liberal accounts of Islam as lacking
in individualism, while simultaneously condemnatory of Islamist resistance
to passing off, which he brands as pathological or as suffering from some
form of 'group delirium' [*délire collectif*] (ibid., p. 49). In another related
but earlier context, he makes a policy recommendation for Arab pedagogy
through cautioning that unless the Arabs 'introduce Kant's critique of
pure reason into their educational curricula, they would be committing a
horrendous error' (Benslama & Quybasi 2008, p. 15).

Herein lies the importance of the discourse of scientism and rationalism
with which Benslama identifies modernity, the West, and psychoanalysis to
which he opposes Islamism (in the singular, despite his own assertions that
it is a plural phenomenon (Benslama 2002, pp. 24–5)) and the one Islam. He
consecrates a series of binaries to make this opposition clear:

> This line does not only pass between those who are tolerant and those who are
> fanatical, between rationalists and believers, between the logic of science and
> the logic of faith, but also between the position that thinks it can find the truth
> of origin in the texts of tradition – and this position thinks that this could be
> done through rational procedures armed with the good speech of the historical
> method – and the position that considers these same texts as a fiction or as a
> legend. (Benslama 2002, p. 36)

In this regard, it is most perplexing that Benslama discusses some
Islamists' attempt to make the Qur'anic text correspond to scientific
knowledge as a sort of neurosis or more precisely as 'interpretative delirium'
[*délire interprétative*], and not part of their rationalization of religion (ibid.,
p. 70). He adds that 'examining these [Islamist] documents leaves one
with the impression of an immense interpretative delirium, ushered in
from a destruction anxiety and constituting an attempt to repair from
the outside that which has collapsed on the inside' (ibid.). This is ironic,
given Benslama's commitment to rationalism and the fact that he chose
the non-ironically named 'Association of Arab Rationalists', of which he
is a member, to publish the Arabic translation of his book. Benslama's
use of these taxonomies of rationalism and irrationalism, science and faith,
knowledge or ignorance, is in fact shared by many among Islamist thinkers.
If the Islamist thinker Sayyid Qutb referred to his contemporary Muslims
and non-Muslims as still living in an age of ignorance (echoing the Qur'an's
description of the pre-Islamic period), Benslama, aside from using post-
Enlightenment descriptions of 'darkness' and 'obscurantism' to characterize

Islamists, insists that Muslim men of religion live 'in great ignorance' (Benslama & Quybasi 2008, p. 18).

The opposition of science to religion and the correlate characterization of psychoanalysis as a 'science' that is opposed by Islam as 'religion' is shared among many of Benslama's psychoanalytic colleagues, including Tarabishi, Safouan and, more recently, Adnan Hoballah. Here, the reification of psychoanalysis as science and the elision of the important debates within psychoanalysis about its own scientificity, let alone Freud's own overdetermined relationship to science, are never acknowledged or referenced by any of them. Perhaps, Benslama's resistance to, or anxiety about, the possibility of many *psychoanalyses* rather than one true psychoanalysis parallels his anxiety about the one Islam and the many. Still, these thinkers differ among themselves about the nature of the relationship between 'Islam' and science. This opposition is not new but harks back to Orientalist Ernest Renan's infamous debate with Jamal al-Din al-Afghani in the 19th century about this very question, wherein Islam and the Arabs were castigated as 'hostile to science' – a debate with which none of these thinkers seems familiar (Massad 2008, pp. 11–16).

Benslama has a major concern with the liberal notion of tolerance, which he finds lacking in the one Islam propagated by the Islamists (all of them?), but which he seems to think is in abundance in European rationalism and secularism (all of it?). Here Benslama's commitment to liberalism is also a commitment to the Freudian equation of individualism with phylogenetic and ontogenetic maturity to which Freud opposes group solidarity and organicism as primitive and regressive, *and* a commitment to Freud's consideration of tolerance as marking the highest maturity achieved by liberal political orders, which are essentially synonyms for high civilization. Freud's accounts of these questions, as Wendy Brown (2006) has shown, can be read in two different directions, as both how men overcome primitive asociality towards forms of social life free from strife in a social contractarian manner (*Civilization and Its Discontents* and *Totem and Taboo*), and as the overcoming of primitive solidarity and organicism to achieve civilized individuality (*Group Psychology and the Analysis of the Ego*). In contrast, liberal notions insist that civilized individualist liberal tolerance, as Brown put it: 'is only available to liberal subjects and liberal orders and constitute the supremacy of both over dangerous alternatives. They also establish organicist orders as a natural limit of liberal tolerance, as intolerable in consequence of their own intolerance' (Brown 2006, p. 303). Thus, while Benslama chastises the one Islam and Islamists (always seen as deploying one singular meaning and interpretation of the one Islam) for lacking any rationalism or tolerance, and that he wants to deny them any tolerance as a consequence of their own alleged intolerance, he wants to extend tolerance to the individualist Islam he rescues from (all) the Islamists and from the Orientalists as one that can feature this important civilized value. In this sense, his liberal values differ little from the general understanding that liberalism has of societies who insist on different forms of sociality and which it considers other. As Brown maintains: 'Organicist orders are not only radically other to liberalism but betoken the "enemy within" civilization and the enemy to civilization. Most dangerous of all would be transnational formations imagined as organicist from a liberal perspective, which link the two – Judaism in the nineteenth century, communism in the twentieth, and today, of course, Islam' (Brown 2006, p. 310). Here the historic links between liberal anti-Semitism and Orientalism and liberal anti-communism are shown to inhabit the very same politics of identity and othering.

I should note here, though, that Judaism, having entered after World War II the liberal Western dyad identified as 'Judeo-Christian' civilization, now mostly escapes such descriptions, save for those Judaisms that resist their inclusion in this liberal order. Indeed, Benslama himself was implicitly so impressed with the Jewish achievement of Western liberalism (i.e. Jews having reached Western liberal individual maturity), which he wants Muslims to emulate, that he exaggerates the scientific achievement of Jews by endowing Christian thinkers with Jewish identities. In his rush to demonstrate his defence of the Europeanized and therefore liberal, mature, and Enlightened 'Jews' against a fantasized primitive obscurantist Arab anti-Jewishness that could explain what he considers to be an 'Arab' or 'Muslim' rejection of psychoanalysis as the 'Jewish science' – a European notion which in fact has little resonance among Arab or Muslim thinkers – Benslama responds thus:

> I feel some shame when I find myself having to draw attention to the fact that he who thinks like this must also deny the theory of gravity or the theory of relativity, which were both the result of the work of Jewish scientists, Newton and Einstein. (Benslama & Quybasi 2008, p. 14)

It seems Benslama is not only unfamiliar with the fact that Newton was Christian, but also with the latter's major exegetical contributions to Christian theology. His exaggeration of Jewish achievements and Arab failures recalls his preference for Isaac over Ishmael noted earlier.

In reading Benslama, one gets the general sense that psychoanalytic studies of Islamists (seen in their entirety as upholding the one illiberal Islam) replicate ego psychology's methods of looking for the neurotic mechanisms in the childhood of a person that prevents him and her from accepting authority and joining the call of normativity. Islamist and Muslim resistance to Western secular and liberal (read Christian) normativity is seen as psychic resistance to maturity and to adult authority, and a rebellion against normativity. Like American imperialism, a liberal civilizational psychoanalysis, of the sort Benslama promotes, seeks to bring these recalcitrant and sick elements back into society and nurse them back to good health. It is unclear if Benslama's political and physical location in France, like the rest of his cohort, might account for this type of liberalism (although it does certainly explain his sense of 'shame'), but it could at least contextualize the kind of critiques with which he wants to engage and in which he wants to insert his own.

Two trends are juxtaposed in Benslama's text, a condemnation of a static Islamic theology, which he declares 'fossilized by centuries of immobility' (Benslama 2002, p. 43), and a break with Islamic origins that modernity – through colonialism – has ushered in the Muslim world, which brought about the one Islam in reaction to it. Based on his research, Benslama diagnoses the situation today as follows: 'What has happened in Islam in the last twenty odd years emerges from this conjuncture; it proceeds from a break which cuts its history and opens inside it another possibility of history' (ibid., p. 317). His findings while researching 'the transformation of the figure of the father and of the paternal function' in a Tunis suburb in the mid-1980s were sufficient for him to recognize that there was a 'deeper' and 'more longstanding' dis-ease ['malaise'] afflicting 'Islamic civilization', and not merely one suburb (Benslama 2004a, p. 76). It is unclear if this is on account of Benslama's or his Tunisian subjects' symbolic conflation of the father and the paternal function with Islam as one and the same! This would be significant because Benslama spends some time in his book correctly pointing out that, unlike in Christianity, God in 'Islam' has no paternal role at all to play and indeed such a role is explicitly repudiated in the Qur'an. Benslama blames Arab and Muslim intellectuals and the political elite for the dis-ease from which Islam seems to suffer: 'an elite that did not know how to translate the modern to the public, nor utilize the interpretative and political possibilities to moderate the public's excesses' (Benslama 2002, pp. 317–18). His conclusion that in the Arab world 'modernity was not therefore but a simulacrum of the modern' (ibid., p. 318) betrays a belief that 'modernity' in the West is a fact, rather than an interpretation.

Even though Benslama insists that 'Islamism [again seen as a phenomenon with one singular meaning and referent] does not sum up Islam [but which Islam?]' (ibid., p. 319), he maintains that analyzing these destructive effects on the break [césure] should not serve an essentialist process which would in turn ignore the contemporary historical and material forces that have led Islam to 'be out of joint' (ibid.). The work of culture, he continues, has difficulty thinking through this 'deracination' of Muslims from their own history in their encounter with the simulacrum of modernity. It is 'this transgression, about which nothing is said, that has determined here the task of the psychoanalyst' (ibid.). Yet, at the end of the book and after he presents the reasons for why Islamism should be read under erasure, we are reminded that 'one cannot exonerate Islam of this ideology' of Islamism (ibid., p. 318)! This tension between the one Islam and the many informs Benslama's discussion throughout.

But there is a resolution to this tension. Understanding that the only way out of the one Islam is the way into liberal secularism, Benslama has more recently co-founded 'The Association of the Manifesto of Freedoms' and is signatory to (author of?) its founding declaration. It is noteworthy that the vocabulary that informs the declaration is borrowed wholesale from American cold-war anti-communism. The declaration affirms that its members who are 'holders of the values of secularism and of sharing a common world ...[are] linked by our own individual histories, and in different ways, to Islam ... ', which the declaration defines 'as a place where many of the dangers of a globalized world crystallize: identitarian fascism and a totalitarian hold, civil and colonial wars, despotisms and dictatorships, inequality and injustice, self-hatred and hatred of the other, amidst political, religious, and economic extremes' (Benslama 2004b, pp. 91–2). Islamists (all of them?) are said to constitute 'forces of destruction' that must be opposed through democracy and the institution of the political, which cannot be imposed militarily but must 'target the internal structures of Islam [but, again, which Islam?] and modify its relations to its geopolitical borders' (ibid., p. 92). While a singular Islam (which seems to be the only state in which Islam can exist at present, according to Benslama's reading) is being singled out in the declaration for this transformation, the signatories insist that they will fight and resist what they call 'totalitarian Islamism' (ibid., p. 93).

Ironically, not all Islamists oppose psychoanalysis, and some of them are in fact open to it. Unlike Benslama's full-scale rejection of Islam as Islamism (both seen as singular as signifiers and signified), Ahmad al-Sayyid 'Ali Ramadan, an Egyptian professor of psychology teaching in Saudi Arabia, is not only tolerant of Freudian psychoanalysis but offers an Islamist assessment of the positive and negative aspects of it from an 'Islamic' perspective. After reviewing and commenting on the oeuvre of Freud and the psychoanalytic method as well as the history of Western critiques of psychoanalysis and the history of its practice in Egypt, Ramadan concludes with a list of the positive contributions of psychoanalysis, including Freud's concept of the 'unconscious', the method of 'free association', 'releasing the patient's anxieties', 'giving confidence [to the patient]', 'bringing unconscious struggles to the surface of consciousness', 'reducing the resistance' of the patient, the discovery of the 'Oedipus complex', and more (Ramadan 2000, pp. 227–8). Ramadan takes psychoanalysis so seriously that he compares it to the Qur'anic notions of the psyche and shows where they converge and diverge. (ibid., pp. 269–327). My point here is not only to cite the openness of Ramadan to Freudian psychoanalysis, but also to show that Benslama seems not only intolerant of the 'intolerance' of Islamism(s), but also of its *tolerance*.

Benslama, then, like some of the Islamists he decries, but certainly not like others who do not exist in his epistemological framework, wants to fix the many Islams he identifies into one form. For him the only tolerable

Islam is a liberal form of Islam that upholds all the liberal values of European maturity and is intolerant of the Islam of the Islamists whose values are said to oppose liberal values even *when they do not*. He also wants to fix the meaning of Islamism as one that upholds the illiberal Islam, which he cannot tolerate. In Benslama's hands, psychoanalysis becomes the handmaiden of European liberalism that shows no ambivalence about its self or its projected other. On the contrary, the certainty with which 'Islam' is *christened* the other of liberalism and the West aligns it with the figure of the primitive and the pre-oedipal child in the cosmology of Freudian psychoanalysis. Benslama is not alone in effecting this transformation but is rather part of a large group of European and Arab thinkers who are insistent on these representations. While he had brilliantly analysed the figure of Abraham and Ishmael in the Qur'an and the Islamic theological tradition, it is when he wants to deal with contemporary Islamists that his psychoanalytic insights are transformed into invocations of liberalism. It is this liberal identity and the mechanisms through which it produces its others that are taken as uninterrogable referents in his work and in the work of his cohort. This serious limitation of Benslama's oeuvre more generally, however, can be productively read in a psychoanalytic way. Indeed, this might be a great task for psychoanalysis at present, namely to study the processes through which the liberal self is constituted by Europeans and intellectual migrants from the non-European post-colonies. A more curious psychoanalysis, perhaps, would do well to undertake a study of the group psychology of liberal and secular thinkers more generally on the question of 'Islam' to uncover the unconscious processes and mechanisms at play in the formation of their liberal ego, which in turn privileges this liberal reading of something they insist on othering as 'Islam'.

References

Arkun, M (1998) *Tarikhiyyat al-Fikr al-'Arabi al-Islami* [The Historicity of Arab Islamic Thought]. Casablanca: Al-Markhaz al-Thaqafi al-'Arabi.

Asad, M. (1947) *Islam at the Crossroads*. Lahore: Arafat Publications.

Benslama, F. (1988) *La nuit brisée*. Paris: Ramsay.

Benslama, F. (2002) *La psychanalyse à l'épreuve de l'Islam*. Paris: Flammarion.

Benslama, F. (2004a) Une recherche psychanalytique sur l'Islam. *La Célibataire 'La psychanalyse et le monde arabe'* 1(8): 75–84, Printemps.

Benslama, F. (2004b) Déclaration de la fondation de l'Association du Manifeste des libertés. In: *Déclaration d'insoumission à l'usage des musulmans et de ceux qui ne le sont pas*, pp. 91–3. Paris: Flammarion.

Benslama, F. & Qubaysi, H. (2008) Shajarat al-Islam, al-Tahlil al-Nafsi, Al-Huwiyyah. Interview conducted by Husayn Quybaysi with Fethi Benslama, in *Al-Tahlil al-Nafsi wa al-Thaqafah al-'Arabiyyah-al-Islmiyyah*. Damascus: Dar Bidayat.

Bin Salamah, F. (2008) *Al-Islam wa al-Tahlil al-Nafsi*, trans. Dr Raja' Bin Salamah. Beirut: Dar al-Saqi and Rabitat al-'Aqlaniyyin al-'Arab.

Brown, W. (2006) Subjects of tolerance. In: H. De Vries and L.E. Sullivan (eds), *Political Theologies: Public Religions in a Post-Secular World*, pp. 298–317. New York, NY: Fordham University Press.

Eickelman, D.F. & Piscatori, J. (1996) *Muslim Politics*. Princeton, NJ: Princeton University Press.

Freud, S. (1939) *Moses and Monotheism*. In: J. Strachey (ed.), *The Standard Edition of the Complete Psychological Works of Sigmund Freud 1953–1974*, vol. 23, pp. 3–137. London: Hogarth.

Fromm, E. (1950) *Psychoanalysis and Religion*. New Haven, CT: Yale University Press.

Margoliouth, D.S. (1986) *Mohammedanism*. London: Williams & Norgate.

Massad, J. (2008) *Desiring Arabs*. Chicago, IL: University of Chicago Press.

Qutb, S (2005) *Al-Islam wa Mushkilat al-Hadarah* [Islam and the Problems of Civilization]. Cairo: Dar al-Shuruq.

Ramadan, A. (2000) *Al-Islam wa al-Tahlil al-Nafsi 'ind Fruyd* [Islam and Freud's Psychoanalysis]. Al-Mansura, Egypt: Maktabat al-Iman.

Safouan, M. (2007) *Why the Arabs Are Not Free? The Politics of Writing*. Oxford: Blackwell.

Said, E. (2003) *Freud and the Non-European*. London: Verso.

Shakir, M. (1992) *Risalah fi al-Tariq ila Thaqafatina* [A Letter on the Path to Our Culture]. Cairo: Mu'assasat al-Risalah.

Tarabishi, J. (2008) *Hartaqat 2: 'an al-'Ilmaniyyah ka-Ishkaliyyah Islamiyyah-Islamiyyah* [Hereticisms 2: On Secularism as a Muslim–Muslim Problematic]. Beirut: Dar al-Saqi.

Von Grunebaum, G.E. (1955) *Islam. Essays on the Nature and Growth of a Cultural Tradition*. London: Routledge & Kegan Paul.

ABSTRACT

This paper examines the terms and methods used by psychoanalytic authors to explain and understand something they other as 'Islam'. The paper engages critically and psycho-analytically with these authors' attempts to read 'Islam' psychoanalytically, and finds that more often than not they subject it to liberal principles that are not defined in psychoanalytic terms. Focusing on the work of Tunisian author Fethi Benslama, the paper analyses and deconstructs certain key semantic and conceptual confusions of 'Islam' and 'Islamism' that are manifest in the general psychoanalytic literature on 'Islam'.

Key words: Benslama, Islam, Islamism, liberalism, other, psychoanalysis

DOI: 10.3366/E1460823509000403

PROMISED LAND OR PERMITTED LAND: A CONSIDERATION OF JEWISH FUNDAMENTALISM IN THE LIGHT OF LEVINASIAN ETHICS

Stephen Frosh, London, UK

Introduction

Jewish fundamentalism has many sources and variants, including extreme religious Zionism, ultra-orthodox Ashkenazi Zionist rejectionism, Sephardi political fundamentalism, and various modes of Hassidism and non- or anti-Hassidic 'mitnagdim'. Generically, these groups are nowadays referred to by the sobriquet 'haredi', or 'tremblers' (before God) and many of them are enclave communities with their own inward-looking structures and strong community ties, and a suspicious, largely arms-length attitude to the rest of the 'modern' world. The fundamentalist elements of Judaism are by no means restricted to Israel (in the UK, they can be found concentrated in parts of north London and Manchester), and indeed their social and political significance in some areas should not be underestimated (for example, around 25% of the children in one London district are haredi children [Holman & Holman 2002]). However, it is the belligerent religious Zionists in Israel who have the most political significance in the contemporary world, because their strident attitude towards the inviolability of the Land of Israel and their consequent support for the settler movement in the Occupied Territories is a major source of tension and one of the most powerful blocks to the peace process there. Ironically, most orthodox Jews were originally opposed to secular Zionism, however much their prayerful yearnings were directed towards a 'return' to Zion; but after the Shoah and then again after the Six-Day War, the messianic component of orthodoxy has largely been combined with a vision of Israel as potentially the precursor of a full salvation; and in any case, they argue that Torah law prohibits Jews from giving up any of the 'Holy Land', as this

STEPHEN FROSH is Professor of Psychology in the Department of Psychosocial Studies at Birkbeck College, University of London. His books include *Hate and the Jewish Science: Nazism, Anti-Semitism and Psychoanalysis* (Palgrave, 2005). Address for correspondence: School of Psychosocial Studies, Birkbeck, University of London, Malet Sreet, London WC1E 7HX. [s.frosh@bbk.ac.uk]

Psychoanalysis and History 11(2), 2009

would thwart God's plan for the final redemption of the Jewish people. The emotive intensity of this position cannot be overstated: the vast majority of all Jews, whether religious or secular, support the existence of the State of Israel and worry about its security; and whilst much of the hate-filled and xenophobic rhetoric of the settlers is anathema to most Jews, the emotional and to a considerable extent political attachment to the land is not.

It will already be clear that the definition of 'fundamentalism' is no more straightforward in relation to Jews than it would be for any other religious group. In relation to religious Zionism, however, it can be usefully formulated as a justification of conquest of the Land of Israel (a somewhat disputed geographical notion itself, but usually extended to mean what the settlers call 'Judea and Samaria') in the light of what are seen as clear Torah (biblical) statements of the God-given Jewish ownership of this land. Indeed, fundamentalist religious Zionists would go further, to argue that there is a biblical injunction to possess the land and to wipe out all forms of opposition to this – in practice, that ownership of the land is more important than peace. The grounds for this lie in the special covenant of the Jewish people with God, which includes the founding of a Jewish, or perhaps *Judaic*, society in the Holy Land, which because of its religious–historical significance is also a spiritually special place, a higher order of location lifted above its material reality but nevertheless rooted in it.

This issue of the Torah justification for occupation of the Land of Israel cannot just be dismissed as the irrational or bad faith rhetoric of a colonizing group; nor is it helpful to simply write off the religious impulse within this group as an irrelevance in contemporary times. It has to be understood as part of the orthodox Jewish religious tradition, in which sacred texts have a living impact on people's everyday worlds; indeed, the broad understanding of 'fundamentalist' as in 'taking the Bible literally' could be said to have been the dominant feature of pre-emancipation Judaism, if one makes the very important move of including in the idea of 'taking literally' the 'oral law' codified in post-biblical texts (notably the early rabbinic literature, encompassing talmudic and midrashic texts and later commentaries). In this regard, it is worth recalling that in Judaism (as in other religions) all sacred texts require interpretation, and it is the authority of the interpretation which fixes it in place as the legitimate way to read the text. Members of fundamentalist Jewish sects rely on rabbinic interpretations of the written text, constantly reapplied to the demands of contemporary life by the leaders of these sects, albeit based firmly in textual and hermeneutic precedents. This, however, is also an important element in the response one might have to religious fundamentalism, including the particular case of Zionist fundamentalism. The 'texts' do not speak straightforwardly: not only are they always amenable to alternative interpretations but, at least in the Jewish tradition, what one might term a variety of 'subjugated narratives' are retained within the holy texts themselves, as a kind of 'trace', sometimes explicit, sometimes more akin to what one might call 'unconscious' residues. One should not be too idealistic here: Jewish scholarship, for example in the Talmud, is based around argument and dispute, but in every instance such dispute resolves itself into an agreed halacha, or legal ruling, which is what the orthodox will follow. Nevertheless, the existence of debate – indeed the promotion of argument 'for the sake of heaven', i.e. in order to explore the Torah more deeply – is a key aspect of Jewish life and, with the caveat just given, it marks out a space of resistance to fundamentalism: there is no single absolute reading that can be given, no certainty without an undercurrent of doubt. Note here that this is a *religious* justification for an opposition to religious fundamentalism: the reason why the Talmud codifies argument is that humans do not have the capacity to fully understand the Torah, which itself can always be subject to 'seventy interpretations', seventy here being shorthand for infinity. For reasons of community cohesion and religious order, certain readings of the Torah are seen as more legitimate than others, so it is not correct to say that any ruling is only temporary or relativistic. Nevertheless, the Talmud preserves evidence of its debates and uncertainties; these offer leverage for those who are troubled by the apparent definitiveness of the religious world.

There is a further preliminary point to make here, which has to do with the supposed 'chosenness' of the Jewish people. This chosen status is usually understood in relation to the injunction to be a 'light to the nations', a 'kingdom of priests', promoting Torah and its values and leading the world in understanding God's moral vision: the first monotheism, the first democratic approach to justice ('Justice, justice shall you follow' [Deuteronomy 16: 20][1]) and so on. This is an uplifting vision, and one that carries with it a continuing tension within Judaism and amongst many of its most sophisticated thinkers, between a universalistic view of the good of all humanity (after all, Judaism is not evangelical and acknowledges that all people have their own route to God) and a particularist notion of the Jews as having a special role – not one amongst many, but a leading one, giving the Jews special responsibilities and maybe special rights. Even in the sophisticated work of some major philosophers, this point about the special nature of the Jews can become contentious. Freud had this idea, but for him it was produced by the history of the Jewish people which forced them to adopt the values of the mind as a way of managing survival (Freud 1939; Frosh 2005). In the case of the thinker with whom the rest of this paper is concerned, Emmanuel Levinas, the issue is more complex.

Levinas' profound influence on contemporary philosophy (including psychoanalysis) lies largely in his articulation of the foundational status of the 'other' in the construction and ontology of human subjecthood. There is

---

1. The full verse is 'Justice, Justice shall you follow, so that you may live, and inherit the land which the Lord your God gives you.'

no opportunity to deal with this in detail here (see Frosh & Baraitser, 2003); it will have to suffice to say that Levinas makes it clear that a relationship of responsibility towards the other – an ethical relation – is in his view *primary*, rather than following on from something pre-existent. It is not the case that the human subject exists and then engages in ethical relations; rather, ethics is the defining feature of subjectivity itself:

> I speak of responsibility as the essential, primary and fundamental structure of subjectivity. For I describe subjectivity in ethical terms. Ethics, here, does not supplement a preceding existential base; the very node of the subjective is knotted in ethics understood as responsibility. I understand responsibility as responsibility for the Other, thus as responsibility for what is not my deed, or for what does not even matter to me; or which precisely does matter to me, is met by me as face. (Levinas 1985, p. 95)

Levinas insists that responsibility for the other comes before the subject can even know what the other is; it is, consequently, an absolute given, and the recognition which is part of it is as non-contingent as can be. This is caught up, famously and controversially, in Levinas' account of suffering and persecution: the other's actions make demands on the subject, and these demands put the subject in a kind of 'persecuted' position which still produces a requirement of responsibility. That is, the intrusion of the other requires the subject to set aside an egocentric response of self-preservation, creating a demand that the subject maintains an awareness of responsibility for the other, even if and when that other is persecutory. As Judith Butler (2005) points out, this is a troubling philosophy, made even more so when Levinas elides it with a view of 'Israel' (which means both the people and the State, it seems) as especially persecuted: 'The ultimate essence of Israel derives from its innate predisposition to involuntary sacrifice, its exposure to persecution' (Levinas 1990, p. 225[2]). Butler argues that, in making this move, Levinas extracts the 'Jew' from history, presenting the Jew's fate as timelessly one of suffering, and then reads this as also the fate of Israel, making a special case for the position of the Jew, spiritually and politically, and, as Butler puts it (in what is otherwise a rather sympathetic critical analysis of Levinas' philosophy), providing 'an implausible and outrageous account of the Jewish people problematically identified with Israel and figured only as persecuted and never persecuting' (Butler 2005, p. 95). A tension exists here between the universalistic and particularistic elements of what is undoubtedly a profound philosophy, and I want to suggest that this is endemic to the Jewish religious impulse and also gestures towards an unconscious sense of guilt that might be discerned in various Jewish textual traces.

---

2. This paper was first published in the mid-1960s, at about the same time as the Talmudic reading to be discussed below.

Levinas the Jew

The choice of Levinas here is not accidental: he was one of the most significant and influential philosophers of the 20th century, whose work is currently heavily referenced not only in philosophy but also in social theory, the social sciences and psychoanalysis (e.g. Alford 2007; Marcus 2007), and whose undertaking provides a foundation for a philosophy of ethics that can be seen as deeply universalist. On the other hand, as already noted, there are particularist tendencies in Levinas that have provoked controversy, especially in relation to his often outspoken defence of the State of Israel in the face of post-1967 criticism. But there is another element in Levinas' work that is especially well attuned to the debate on – and, it will be argued, the rebuttal of – Jewish fundamentalism. This is his deep engagement with Jewish religious texts and his attempt to explore this material in such a way as to derive meaning from it in a contemporary context. The point here needs to be made strongly: all orthodox Jews derive the legitimation for their actions, their moral and ethical ideas, their understanding of history and culture, and their Jewish identity from texts. Study of the Torah and its interpretation in the early rabbinic literature, alongside a limited number of later commentaries, is a core component of Jewish religious life, every bit as important as – perhaps more important than – prayer. It is from these texts that the orthodox derive the axes that govern their personal and their public lives, including their politics. From a religious point of view, therefore, intervention in the interpretation of these texts is a highly significant way of debating within orthodoxy, of not only doing what Levinas claimed to be doing, translating the Jewish sources into 'Greek', but of reflecting back to Jews themselves.

Levinas' engagement with the Talmud was deep and has probably not been given due attention, although it is by no means unknown. First it is worth recollecting how immersed Levinas was in Jewish life. Born in 1906 into an orthodox family in Kovno, Lithuania, he was brought up reading Hebrew, even though his first spoken language was Russian. In the 1920s and 1930s in France, when he was at his greatest distance from Judaism, he was nevertheless a member of the Alliance Israélite Universelle, an organization with a largely assimilationist programme based on enlightening backward Jews in secular knowledge. However, in the 1930s Levinas was already reconsidering this outlook, seeking ways of returning Jews to their own heritage as a way of accessing the inner sources of their creativity, whilst retaining the orientation towards an emancipatory future. Aronowicz (1990) comments:

> For Levinas, the rethinking of the relation of Jewish to 'Greek' sources would have to include the vision of *universality*, of *one* humanity in which all related as equals and in which all participated responsibly, the ideals of the Alliance. The difference now was that in order for this *one* humanity to come into being,

Western sources of spirituality, Western wisdom, would no longer suffice. In order for a genuine human community to emerge, it was *Jewish* wisdom, the *Jewish* vision of the human being, which must be understood and made available to everyone else. (p. xiii)

For Levinas, therefore, this is the beginning of the strand of his thought that makes the particularity of Judaism essential for the well-being of the world. After the war, this task became yet more urgent and also ambivalent, and was informed by the deep study that Levinas made of the Talmud with his somewhat mysterious teacher, M. Chouchani (also Elie Wiesel's teacher), during the period 1947–51. In 1946, however, Levinas took on what was to be his day job for much of the rest of his life. Rather than being an academic in a university, he became Director of the École Normale Israélite Orientale, an Alliance teacher training college; his professional activity became dedicated to developing an approach which took seriously both the requirements of the world (his 'secular' philosophy) and of Judaism. Jews would need to be open to the world, as Levinas was; Jews would also need to know their culture, their sources, and to utilize this knowledge in the service of the world.

Levinas' Talmudic commentaries reflect this dual aspect: they were not confined to the rooms of the seminary, but instead were given to the annual gatherings of French Jewish intellectuals, the 'Colloques d'intellectuels juifs de langue française' in which he participated from the early 1960s. These readings of Talmudic texts, some of which are gathered together in Levinas' (1990) *Nine Talmudic Readings*, are a considerable achievement. They show him working within the traditions of Talmudic commentary, ostensibly just translating and describing, yet also reading with a contemporary twist, aware of the times and their concerns. They are hermeneutic readings which function to open out texts, in many places uncovering a subversive side-reading or subjugated narrative that produces a troubled surprise in orthodox readers, unable to deny the presence of these textual strands, yet having one's assumptions disrupted. In this way, they are true to a certain tradition not just of Jewish reading, but of *psychoanalytic* reading, in which texts are treated not as transparent productions from the unconscious of a particular author (a once common, but illegitimate use of psychoanalysis in literary criticism), but rather as the site of a struggle that leaves behind traces. Freud gives a suitably dramatic account of this process in one of his own 'religious' tracts, *Moses and Monotheism*, where he describes biblical texts as a kind of covering-over, embodying evidence of an act of violence, even of a crime. He writes:

The text, however, as we possess it today, will tell us enough about its own vicissitudes. Two mutually opposed treatments have left their traces on it. On the one hand it has been subjected to revisions which have falsified it in the sense of their secret aims, have mutilated and amplified it and have even changed it into its reverse; on the other hand a solicitous piety has presided over it and has sought to preserve everything as it was, no matter whether it was consistent or contradicted itself. Thus almost everywhere noticeable gaps, disturbing repetitions and obvious contradictions have come about – indications which reveal things to us which it was not intended to communicate. In its implications the distortion of a text resembles a murder: the difficulty is not in perpetrating the deed, but in getting rid of its traces. (Freud 1939, p. 43)

It is in these 'traces' that the 'unconscious' of the text resides; whether in subtle distortions or visible undercurrents of dispute, religious texts commonly reveal the uncertainties and ambivalences that go into their construction, but are then repressed ('murdered') to produce an acceptable mode of orthodoxy.

In relation to Levinas' Talmudic explorations, the power of such a hermeneutic endeavour is perhaps nowhere more obvious than in the reading concentrated on below, holding in mind the claim of Zionist religious fundamentalists that there is textual proof of their absolute right to the Land of Israel: Levinas' seminar from November 1965 on the section from *Tractate Sotah* concerning the episode of the spies, which is given the title *Promised Land or Permitted Land* (Levinas 1990). My suggestion here is that, albeit in some ways reluctantly and uncertainly, Levinas reveals an undercurrent of doubt in this text that calls into question fundamentalist fervour.[3]

Spying out the Land

The text with which the Talmudic passage is concerned is the account in Numbers and Deuteronomy of the men sent by Moses to spy out the land of Canaan, prior to the planned invasion by the Israelites. The relevance of this to the concerns of Zionist fundamentalists should be obvious, not just in its general subject matter (conquest of the Land of Israel), but in the way the spies are punished for their lack of faith – an early example, one might think, of Jewish self-hatred. The story in brief is that a year after leaving Egypt, and on the borders of Canaan, God tells Moses to send spies into the land, either as a test or simply because the people have been clamouring for this (the version of the story in Deuteronomy has Moses acquiescing to the *people's* demand, with God approving). Twelve spies are sent, one representing each tribe; they go up and down the land, observing its inhabitants and picking its fruits, and come back mightily impressed. It is indeed, they say, a 'land of milk and honey'; the problem is that the people within it are fierce, are giants, and there is little chance of the Jews overcoming them. Only Joshua

---

3. I am neither a real Levinas expert nor a Talmudic expert, so this is an amateur, 'psychoanalytic' reading, wondering about the tensions and ambivalence to be found in Levinas' text and possibly (as he seems to claim) in the original.

and Caleb stand out against this dismal scene, and they are nearly stoned for their trouble until an appearance of the cloud of God saves them. God then threatens to destroy the people because of their ingratitude, which Moses dissuades Him from doing, but the 10 critical spies are killed by a plague, and the people are punished by being condemned to wander in the wilderness for a further 39 years, until all the men (with the exception of Joshua and Caleb) have died out and been replaced by a new generation, more doughty and muscular in its approach to battle, less full of slave mentality.

These are the bones of the story, but as ever the Talmud fleshes it out and introduces numerous issues which are derived from a close reading of the text. One has to remember here that if this is genuinely Holy Writ, as it was for the Talmudic rabbis, then every nuance will have meaning, nothing is accidental or reducible to mere noise; every element of the message is ripe for decoding. In their enthusiastic response to the challenge of opening out the text for associations and disputatious readings, the rabbis are engaging in a *religious* act, as is Levinas in his response. Characteristically, the Talmud moves back and forth between different textual allusions, draws on myths and received opinions, and constructs a narrative which is consciously polysemic, even though it also seeks to present itself as an authoritative rendering of what the Torah means. Levinas has his own take on this, and one can justifiably claim that it is 'just one view'; the argument here is that doing this his way, philosophically, one might say, produces a disruption of set or automatic meaning that makes fundamentalist arguments about the land untenable. Levinas states:

> What seems so simple in the biblical text, the fear which seizes the children of Israel when they are just about to reach their goal, will become problematic in the Talmudic text we are reading. In the great fear of the explorers, we may discover anxieties more familiar to us... You will see... that in the course of history, Jewish thought, like Jewish conscience, has known every scruple, every remorse, even when it came to the most sacred rights of the people troubled by this thought. (1990, p. 54)

This is indeed what happens.

The Talmudic text that Levinas extracts starts with a play on words, a conventional rabbinic as well as psychoanalytic ploy. In Deuteronomy, it states that the spies were sent: 'That they may explore the land for us', using the word '*veyachperu*'. The text quotes Rav Hiyya bar Abba as associating this word with the word '*vechapra*', used in Isaiah to mean 'ashamed' ('The moon will be ashamed and the sun will be confounded'), and on the basis of this, he concludes: 'The explorers sought only the shame of the land'. Levinas reads this as a link with the idea of confounding idolaters (those who worship the sun and moon), and from there those who idolize the earth, the land. He concludes (and recall that this was in 1965, before the criticisms of Israel provoked after the Six-Day War):

> The explorers go toward this land so that the land will be shamed, so that the
> worshipers of this land – for example, the Zionists of that time – will be shamed.
> They have decided, in the name of truth, to confound the Zionists. (Levinas 1990,
> p. 56)

The introduction of 'Zionists' at this moment is something of a shock,
suggesting that Levinas is speaking more to his audience than from his
material, wrestling it into becoming a contemporary resource. He clarifies
his point immediately, after an apology for intellectualism ('The intellectual
has been defined as the one who always misses the mark but who, at least,
aims very far'). Levinas claims that in this passage: 'We are informed of the
intention of a few men to put to shame all those who want and hope for the
Promised Land. The Promised Land would not be allowed.' This is a central
idea in Levinas' reading of the Talmudic passage, and he develops it as he
goes along, bringing it into tension with the more traditional notion that
the spies suffered a crisis of faith, but also seeing a deliberate, even ironic
undercurrent to the rabbis' discussions, one which supports the subversive
reading more than it does the orthodox one.

The next part of this has to do with names. The list of names of the spies
is famously hilarious – sons of horse and camel being amongst them – but
the Talmudic text claims (in the name of Rav Isaac) that: 'We have a
tradition according to which the explorers are named after their actions, but
we only know how to interpret one name, that of Sethur, son of Michael'
(p. 56). According to Rav Isaac, he is named Sethur because 'he has given
the lie to [*sathar*] the words of the Holy One Blessed be He' and his
father, Michael, was so called 'because he has weakened him [*mak*]' (p. 51).
Rav Jonathan adds another interpretable name: 'Nahbi, son of Vophsi,
because he hid [*hihbi*] the words of the Holy One. Son of Vophsi because he
jumped over [*pasa*] the attributes of the Holy One, Blessed be He.' Levinas
points out several things about this passage. First its surface meaning: the
fault of the spies includes that they disdain the power of God, who is in
their eyes a 'weak God' who cannot do anything or deliver on his promises,
and in any case he promises nothing, 'He has promised nothing and does
not care at all if virtue is rewarded and vice punished' – this being the
essential attribute of God that the spies 'jump over' (p. 51). But, more
importantly, Levinas shows how the Talmudic discussion of the names is
so blatantly misleading that one is led to ask what truth is being hidden *in
order that* it might be discovered – what trace is there in the text (the closest
we can get to a 'textual unconscious') of something else it might be wanting
to say?

> Read these names. Does one need a tradition to understand the virtues registered
> in these names? One need only think about the roots of these words and show less
> imagination than that which drew from Vophsi 'he-who-jumped-over!' Shammua
> ben Zaccur: he who listens, son of he who remembers; Shaphat ben Hori: he
> who judges, son of he who is free; Igal ben Joseph: the redeemer, son of Joseph;

Palti ben Rafu: he who spares, son of he who was healed. I cannot indulge in this etymological game on all twelve names, but I understand why those who upheld that our explorers were corrupt from birth preferred to forget the tradition! What a lucky amnesia! They found *mak* in Michael but forgot that Michael means 'Who is like God'... All the noble meanings of the names of the guilty were miraculously lost! Don't we have here an effort to remove the suspicion that this whole hateful conspiracy was a plot of the righteous? (Levinas 1990, p. 58)

So the Talmud resists or represses the honourable elements of the spies, but does so with such blatant dissimulation that it actually draws attention to the counter-narrative, one in which righteous men go down to explore the land, and see something there that makes them fear to become settlers. What this 'failure of the righteous' might be is examined in the next remarkable group of passages, but even here one must remember the end of the story, as Levinas does: the spies, whether righteous or not, were punished, the 'halacha' is that they should have gone down. Yet, at what cost, with what ambivalence and uncertainty?[4]

The next section of the Talmudic passage deals with Caleb and his visit to Hebron. It begins with a classic Talmudic worry about a grammatical error in the biblical text, which states (Numbers 13: 22): 'They went toward the South and he came to Hebron.' The rabbis' interpretation of this is that the different spies went to different places, and specifically Caleb went to Hebron, where he prayed at the graves of the patriarchs for protection from the guiles and persuasions of his compatriots, or, as Levinas puts it: 'God, preserve me from my friends' (p. 58). Hebron, we know today as well as then, is and was a place of great contestation, one of the flash-points of the Israel–Palestine conflict, a scene of tragedy on all sides. Here, Caleb is placing himself in the tradition of his ancestors, of Abraham, Isaac and Jacob who are buried there, and seeking support from them for the holy project of conquering the land. Can anything be clearer as a signal from the Talmud of the value given to the tradition that makes the Land of Israel Jewish? As Levinas points out, the next section of the Talmud, which emphasizes the hugeness of the inhabitants of the land, that they were 'descendents of Anak', that is, giants, supports the standard reading of the passage as

---

4. Adam Taub (email of 5 October 2008) objects to this reading on the following grounds: 'Levinas suggests that the obvious misinterpretation of the names implies that the Rabbis are highlighting the high moral standing of the spies that the literal interpretation of the names suggests. In this sense, the Rabbis are using irony as a contra-indicating tool. I find this hard to accept because I don't see irony used in this way by the Rabbis in other places. There are plenty of places where the Rabbis interpret names and actions in ways that fly in the face of the literal meaning in order to paint villains black, e.g. when Esau hugs Yaakov, the Midrash comments that Esau tried to bite Jacob's neck and God turned it to marble. Following Levinas' approach, we should read this as the Rabbis underlining Esau's generosity of spirit.'

revealing the fear of the slave-people confronted with the armed might of the native population. How could a people so recently oppressed believe that they could ever defeat such a powerful enemy? Caleb pleads that the faith of his ancestors will sustain him in the face of this political and military reality. That is, his view, apparently approvingly indexed by the Talmud, is that the religious and moral superiority of the Jews, their direct connection with God through the act of choosing and being chosen, entitles them to pursue the fulfilment of an already-then ages-old promise to Abraham, to inherit the land; and that it is fear alone that one should fear.

But nothing is unequivocal here. In this moment of the insistence of moral superiority, it is not clear who occupies the moral high ground: Levinas comments: 'Perhaps the explorers had moral qualms' (p. 61). The Talmud takes an apparently innocent biblical line and worries away at it, as it always does when faced with the question of explaining why something that seems to be unnecessary has been included in the text: 'Hebron was founded seven years before Zoan' (Numbers 13: 22). So what? Again, the issue is peculiarly Talmudic: how could Hebron, in Canaan, have been founded before Zoan, in Egypt, when a father will always provide for his elder son before his later son; and it states clearly in the Bible in Genesis 10: 6: 'The descendents of Ham: Cush, Mizraim, Put and Canaan'. That is, Ham's son Mizraim (Egypt) was older than Canaan, so Zoan must have been founded before Hebron. Perhaps it means that Hebron was more cultivated than Zoan; yet again this is contradicted by biblical texts, which teach clearly that Hebron is full of rocks (which is why we find a burial place in a cave there) whilst Egypt was fertile ('Like the garden of the Lord, like the land of Egypt', the Talmud quotes from Genesis 13: 10). Hebron, indeed, has one physical claim – because it is barren, it is full of sheep, and the Talmud quotes from the book of Samuel (2 Samuel 15: 7) that Absalom, King David's son, went there to find sheep for his sacrifices. But this is hardly enough to establish Hebron's precedence, so it must mean that the superiority of Hebron, its status as 'before Zoan', is given not by its antiquity or ecology – not, that is, by something physical – but by the special *spiritual* nature of the place. That is, the Holy Land is on a different level, its priority is clearly a religious one, it has a potential which, once realized, is transformative, and because of this: 'Despite the rocks, despite the vast quantity of sand, this country holds more possibilities than Zoan, which is located in the midst of Egypt, in the midst of civilization; it calls upon those who are capable of realizing these potentials. Aren't some rights conferred though moral superiority?' (pp. 62–3). This would be the textual justification for settling but Levinas undermines the claim immediately ('But one can also doubt that moral superiority, of whatever kind, permits an expropriation' [ibid.]), and then goes on to show how delightfully and seditiously the Talmud has subverted its own apparently clear moral justification for colonization. The trick lies

in the exact examples picked by the rabbis in justifying the special status of
Hebron. First, the choice of Ham as the authoritative father who does the
right thing by his children, placing them in order. Surely this is ironic: Ham,
as we know clearly, was damned for shaming his father.[5] Then, of all people,
Absalom, who went to Hebron not solely to worship, but to plot, to unite
people in a revolt against his father. Levinas draws the conclusion:

> Earlier, we had said: We, the Israelites, have a right to this land because we have
> the Bible. The objection consists in reminding us of the very teaching of this Bible
> and the deeds it relates. People of the Book? Nothing but sons who honour their
> fathers? Children who obey all the moral principles? What about Absalom? The
> example is wonderfully well chosen. Bad lots are not lacking in the Bible, but isn't
> Absalom in a certain sense the counterpart of Ham, the founder of the land of
> Canaan? Remember what Ham did. He made fun of his father's nakedness. And
> Absalom? Here a euphemism is in order, even in the presence of intellectuals: he
> cohabited with all his father's concubines on the roof of the royal palace. So much
> for the superiority of Judaism! Which obviously gives it the right to conquer a
> country! One can understand the explorers, one can understand the revolt of the
> pure. They asked themselves ... By what right are we going into this land? What
> moral advantage do we have over the inhabitants settled in this country? (p. 63)

This is a very strong and clear statement, both on behalf of the Talmud,
which slips in its own harmonics, its own associative network, to block a
fundamentalist reading of the right-to-the-Land variety, and by Levinas,
who reinstates doubt in the modern context of the debate over Palestine. In
the rest of the commentary, Levinas heightens this still further, examining
what it means to be involved in a moral crusade and identifying the
quandary of the spies as 'those of an overly pure conscience. It begins
to doubt God because God's command asks us either what is above our
strength or what is beneath our conscience' (p. 64). Like the spies, caught
in the dilemma of how to obey God whilst also obeying their conscience,
Levinas revolves between the positions that there is a moral entitlement to
the land given by the religious particularity of the Jews and that this kind
of entitlement does not actually entitle one to anything. On the one hand,
he uses some of the text to argue for the 'disproportion that exists between
messianic politics and all other politics' (p. 65) and that the act of founding
a 'just' – that is, Torah – community 'sacralizes' the earth, so the pursuit of
Torah is its own legitimating performance:

---

5. Jeremy Schonfield (email of 7 October 2008) comments: 'The Torah also says that
Canaan will always be a slave, but EL doesn't note this. Incidentally, the rabbinic view
was that Canaan, as a descendant of Ham, had no business living in the region of Shem,
and that the land of Canaan was merely being held in trust until Abraham, a Shemite,
would be able to take charge. Rashi in the first verse of Genesis talks about the way God
distributes and redistributes land.'

> What we call the Torah provides norms for human justice. And it is in the name
> of this universal justice and not in the name of some national justice or other that
> the Israelites lay claim to the land of Israel. (p. 66)

On the other hand, Levinas also argues for the limits of this view: quoting
his own translation, he notes that the Talmudic passage states in the name of
Rav Hanina bar Papa (and hence, approvingly): 'Even the Boss, so to speak,
cannot remove his tools from there' (p. 53). That is, in contemporary terms:

> The right of the native population to live is stronger than the moral right of the
> universal God. Even the Boss cannot retrieve the tools entrusted to them; as long
> as the tools correspond to their needs, there would be no right on earth that could
> deprive them of them, one cannot take away from them the land on which they
> live, even if they are immoral, violent, and unworthy and even if this land were
> meant for a better destiny. (p. 67)

This, too, is a strong statement, but one has to remember the end of the
story and of the commentary before hailing the Talmud as a pro-Palestinian
text and calling on Levinas as one of its greatest recent interpreters. In
the former case, the Talmud reminds us that the spies died of the plague,
an 'unnatural death', in which 'their tongue was elongated and reached
down to their navel and... worms issued from the navel to the tongue and
from the tongue to the navel' (p. 54). Or maybe it was 'diphtheria'. They
should have obeyed and encouraged the people to conquer. In Levinas'
case, too, despite his exploration of the undercurrent in the Talmud, he
comes down in the end to the question of faith: 'What matters is the idea of
two punishments' reflecting the two possible reasons for their 'fault': they
might have thought they were too weak, or that the Promised Land was not
permitted to them. 'In both cases,' he writes, 'they were wrong ... ' (p. 69).

A Final Ambivalence

Levinas' reading of the Talmudic passage is both revelatory and
symptomatic. It convincingly plays the rabbis at their own game, using
the clues they give to find the 'unconscious' traces in the text through
associations and harmonics, through word-play and memory, to find another
track in their argument to the one that might have been expected. Rather
than a clear admonition of the religious weakness of the spies and a
justification of their punishment – a straightforward, literal rendering of the
biblical verses – we are offered a subtle examination of human uncertainty,
of fear perhaps mixed with a moral sensibility that is rehearsed constantly
today amongst many mainstream supporters of Israel: with what right does
this or that occur, what are the limits of what is permitted and what is
justifiable? In the end, the rabbis do their job and plump for religious
authority and acceptance, but at times it is a close run thing, and the
beauty of the Talmud is that it allows its readers access to the other, to the

alternatives, the paths less taken, as it were, the undercurrent that does not justify, but questions whether what occurred – and occurs daily – was and is right.[6] For Levinas, too, one might hazard, this was a complex, ambivalent enterprise. On the one hand, a belief in the special position of the Jew and the Torah, and a political and personal commitment to the preservation of the State of Israel. On the other hand, a universalist philosophy in which ethics is the founding of ontology, in which the other is first, and in which it is even or 'especially' the other with whom one has no particular connection, or even the other against whom one is opposed, that one has the most responsibility for. How does one reconcile this particularism and this universalism, this wish to have security and this desire to be an ethical being? The question of 'ethical violence', as we know, is very much in the frame these days (e.g. Butler 2005), and is in part a struggle over whether ethics is part of a humanistic domain of responsibility to the other, or whether it trumps such a code. Here, in Levinas and maybe also in the Talmud, this question is forced shut through a final acceptance of the truth of God's word; but quite a lot of light is let in too, to suggest that there is plenty of room for doubt.

What might be the source of this doubt, psychoanalytically speaking? If the fundamentalist impulse is interpretable at times as a response to anxiety, to the fragmentation or assault on selfhood that comes from the uncertainties endemic to modernity, then the security given by a direct and firm reading of the sacred texts can be understood as a way of bolstering this response, of securing the stability of boundaries and boundedness – itself also a link with the security offered by an obsession with the land. But for a certain kind of modern sensibility, perhaps definable as humanistic or even 'liberal', with all the difficulties of both those words, adoption of the fundamentalist defence itself produces anxiety and, alongside this, guilt. It is not possible to move from the textual traces of the Talmud to suggest that the rabbis felt guilty about the displacement of other people from the land; in any case, this seems unlikely even if the reading that finds guilt feelings amongst the spies is a supportable one. It is also not possible to label the modern, post-Shoah consciousness of the universalist but Jewish-identified Levinas as 'guilty' on the basis of his Talmudic argument; one has to be cautious about sweeping psychoanalytic claims based only on textual and not on face-to-face encounters (and Levinas is the great philosopher of the face-to-face, as Freud – despite his aversion to being looked at – was

---

6. More traditional readers of Talmud have plenty of grounds for objection here. Adam Taub (op. cit.) argues: 'I can't help feeling that Levinas is anxiously seeking something which may not be there. Through ingenious means he suggests that Rabbis of the Talmud were aware of the moral dilemma of settling the land, but I have to wonder if this is the case. I am not sure that the Rabbis had a problem with forced conquest and expulsion – after all they supported (and fought in) three rebellions against Rome with precisely that intent.'

its great psychologist). Still, in his to-ing and fro-ing, in his choice of an obviously colonizing passage to find an emancipatory ethical stance, in finding a meaning under the meaning, and in speaking out publicly but slightly hiddenly about the *religious* problem of identification with Zionist fundamentalism, one might think that Levinas is putting his finger on a specifically Jewish problematic, of how to make claims for something whilst also renouncing those same claims, of how, that is, to live with ambivalence without being overwhelmed by guilt. The ethical stance that Levinas pushes for thus perhaps mirrors the ethical claims of Judaism, all too easily swamped by the stridency of its equally strong, but less legitimate, fundamentalist tendencies.

And, finally, something else is made impossible by this reading. The Jewish fundamentalist claim, with which this paper began, that the Land of Israel is God-given, that the right to it is established beyond doubt by the Bible and reinforced by the inspired texts of Judaism, is made much more muddy and less tenable when one realizes that even the rabbis were not sure. Is it weakness to resist the colonizing impulse, is it a mode of Jewish self-disbelief or even self-hatred? Or is it a moral stance that doubts one's own worthiness and wonders if even the conviction of having *a* right to the land, or possibly of being 'chosen' for a specific role, is sufficient to justify attacks on 'the right of the native population to live'? From a religious perspective, that is, in which one accepts as true some fundamental principles of belief, in our context specifically acceptance of the truth of the Torah and its interpretations through the sages of old, it is still wrong to adopt a fundamentalist position that brooks no opposition. The opposition is there *in the sacred texts themselves* and in the equally sacred activity of interpreting them; one's religious duty, that is, is in part to live in awe of the complexity of reasons and motivations, of justifications and legitimations, which give rise to the actions that we take. This is not so far, of course, from a psychoanalytic sensibility, which also, one might hope, opposes fundamentalism through its awareness of the subversive disruptions that any 'text' might allow.

References

Alford, C.F. (2007) Levinas, Winnicott, and therapy. *Psychoanalytic Review* 9: 529–51.

Aronowicz, A. (1990) Introduction. In: E. Levinas, *Nine Talmudic Readings*. Bloomington, IN: Indiana University Press.

Butler, J. (2005) *Giving an Account of Oneself*. Bronx, NY: Fordham University Press.

Freud, S. (1939) *Moses and Monotheism*. SE 23, pp. 1–137. London: Hogarth, 1964.

Frosh, S. (2005) *Hate and the Jewish Science: Anti-Semitism, Nazism and Psychoanalysis*. London: Palgrave.

Frosh, S. & Baraitser, L. (2003) Thinking, recognition and otherness. *Psychoanalytic Review* 90: 771–89.

Holman, C. & Holman, N. (2002) *Torah, Worship and Acts of Loving Kindness: Baseline Indicators for the Charedi Community in Stamford Hill.* Leicester: De Montfort University.

Levinas, E. (1985) *Ethics and Infinity.* Pittsburgh, PA: Duquesne University Press.

Levinas, E. (1990) *Nine Talmudic Readings.* Bloomington, IN: Indiana University Press.

Marcus, P. (2007) 'You are, therefore I am': Emmanuel Levinas and psychoanalysis. *Psychoanalytic Review* 94: 515–27.

ABSTRACT

Jewish fundamentalism (a contested term that does not sit easily with the non-literal nature of much rabbinic reading of the Bible) has many sources and variants, but amongst these the most belligerent is the mode of fundamentalism expressed by some 'strictly orthodox' Jews in Israel. These Jews tend to justify their continued agitation for a 'greater Israel', accompanied by hostility not only towards Palestinians but also towards secular and politically more liberal Jews, in terms of literalist readings of Torah. This paper approaches this topic 'sideways' (and hence, perhaps, psychoanalytically) through tracking a remarkable reading by Emmanuel Levinas of the Talmudic passage dealing with the biblical account of the spies sent by Moses to Canaan. Levinas' ambivalent shifts between understanding these spies as motivated by an ethical refusal to see themselves as having a right to the land, and seeing them (more conventionally) as having too little faith, perhaps reflects the operations of a 'guilt' about which psychoanalysis may have something to say.

Key words: ambivalence, ethics, Levinas, Jewish fundamentalism, Zionism

DOI: 10.3366/E1460823509000415

SLAYING DRAGONS: MOHSIN HAMID DISCUSSES
THE RELUCTANT FUNDAMENTALIST

Mohsin Hamid, London, UK

This is a daunting audience and a daunting topic. Never before have I felt as exposed on the question of fiction or autobiography. I am going to insist this is fiction and whatever learned members of the audience determine about the psychosis of the characters involved, they have nothing to do with me. The novel *The Reluctant Fundamentalist* (Hamid 2007) is a dramatic monologue, which means it is almost like a stage-play with one character speaking. One reason for having this formal structure is that by creating half of a conversation, a conversation of which you only hear one half, and where the other party of the conversation is only present as an echo, a space opens up in the novel, a vacuum that the reader is invited to fill. *The Reluctant Fundamentalist* plays a kind of game where Changez, the narrator, a Pakistani man with a beard, comes upon an American man with a crew-cut in a bazaar in Lahore, in Pakistan, and starts speaking to him. It is unclear why Changez is deciding to speak to this American or why the American is there, or what has brought them together. Is one a terrorist, a fundamentalist? Is the other a CIA agent, a killer? Are they both two random chaps who happen to be in the bazaar? We don't know and that lack of knowledge and that half conversation does a few things, such as drawing attention to biases. So in non-fiction accounts and narratives, such as the news on television, we tend to be told how things are and, of course, in being told, we are being given a whole string of biases; but the biases remain hidden. But when it is a conversation where one person is speaking and the other person isn't, it is drawing attention to the fact that what you are about to get is very highly biased and manipulative. And you, the audience, are given the task of responding to this manipulation. So the character Changez is in the novel only half a character, and you, the reader, flesh out what that

MOHSIN HAMID is a novelist and journalist. He is the author of *Moth Smoke* (Farrar, Straus & Giroux, 2000) and *The Reluctant Fundamentalist* (Penguin, 2007) which was shortlisted for the Man Booker prize. Address for correspondence: c/o The Freud Museum, 20 Maresfield Gardens, London NW3 5SX.

character is. I will read from the first couple of pages – just to give you a
sense of how it sounds. This is Changez's voice:

> Excuse me, sir, but may I be of assistance? Ah, I see I have alarmed you. Do
> not be frightened by my beard: I am a lover of America. I noticed that you were
> looking for something; more than looking, in fact you seemed to be on a mission,
> and since I am both a native of this city and a speaker of your language, I thought
> I might offer you my services.
>
> How did I know you were American? Not by the colour of your skin; we have
> a range of complexions in this country, and yours occurs often among the people
> of our northwest frontier. Nor was it your dress that gave you away; a European
> tourist could as easily have purchased in Des Moines your suit, with its single vent,
> and your button-down shirt. True, your hair, short-cropped, and your expansive
> chest – the chest, I would say, of a man who bench-presses regularly, and maxes
> out well above two-twenty-five – are typical of a certain type of American; but
> then again, sportsmen and soldiers of all nationalities tend to look alike. Instead,
> it was your bearing that allowed me to identify you, and I do not mean that as an
> insult, for I see your face has hardened, but merely an observation.
>
> Come, tell me, what were you looking for? Surely, at this time of day, only one
> thing could have brought you to the district of Old Anarkah – named, as you may
> be aware, after a courtesan immured for loving a prince – and that is the quest for
> the perfect cup of tea. Have I guessed correctly? Then allow me, sir, to suggest my
> favourite among these many establishments. Yes, this is the one. Its metal chairs
> are no better upholstered, its wooden tables are equally tough, and it is, like the
> others, open to the sky. But the quality of its tea, I assure you, is unparalleled.
> (Hamid 2007, pp. 1–2)

And that is how it begins. Changez starts telling this American the story
of how he got to America, to Princeton University, graduating at the top of
his class, getting a job at a corporate firm engaged in valuing other firms.
Changez spends much of the novel figuring out if he feels comfortable,
morally, with this financial attribution of value by discounting future cash
flows and looking at economic fundamentals. But initially he is very excited
to be top of his class and to be doing very well. I won't say much more about
the American and Changez right now, because I want actually to focus on
Changez himself.

One thing I will say is that, due to the framing narrative, *The Reluctant
Fundamentalist* has often been described as a thriller. But nothing thrilling
really happens in it, although there is of course a lot of smoke and mirrors.
Changez doesn't actually do anything particularly thrilling and neither does
the American. But the reason why I think the novel works to frighten people
is because people are already afraid, so when you encounter a novel where
a sense of fear is being dangled, it gives you hooks on which to hang your
own fear. What the novel tries to do is function as a thriller which mirrors
the pre-existing thrill in the audience and in the reader. We are all afraid
although we know any given conversation is unlikely to end in a shoot-out

or blood-bath. Given the slightest sense in the narrative that something of that nature may potentially take place or that weapons of mass destruction may be found, we tend to indulge ourselves. I won't say more about that, I'll just focus on the story of Changez.

Changez's story is the story of a young man, a college graduate going to work in the corporate world and dealing with being away from home and also falling in love. The woman he's falling in love with is named Erica and they first meet through a friend on a Greek island the summer after he graduates. The interaction between these two characters, Erica and Changez, is problematic on a lot of levels. There is a love triangle in the novel, or maybe a love square or pentagon but at least a love triangle, in which there are Erica and Changez who's from Pakistan – a place he sort of loves but had to leave behind. Erica lives in America and is American, but remains in love with her former boyfriend Chris who has youthfully died of cancer a couple of years before. I hesitate to say the word in front of this audience, but Erica comes across as severely depressed. Erica is close to a pre-20th-century world, to the traditional model of what a lover is supposed to be, according to the model of 'Romeo and Juliet', or of much Pakistani Urdu poetry. It is the notion that you fall in love once, you give up so much of your identity that when your love is over there is no life left to be lived. Previously that sort of pining away to the point of death was a fantastic notion of passionate love. It was even what love was all about, you fell in love and that's how it was. Now, of course, if somebody dies young and you don't recover from their death and bounce back into healthy relationships, you are considered as having some sort of illness. So Erica is this classic in love/ill woman and Changez finds himself trying to win the heart of a woman from a man who is already dead. That of course is an impossible struggle because his competitor can't make any mistakes, he's gone. This affects Changez in a number of ways. But before I take that further and talk about the Changez/Erica relationship I would like to turn to the other dynamic in Changez's life as he's wooing Erica. The corporate world that he is working in around September 11th is hugely affected by September 11th itself and its aftermath. Changez is in the Philippines valuing a company with his firm when September 11th takes place, and I want to read from his reaction to that to give you a sense of what he feels:

> The following evening was supposed to be our last in Manila. I was in my room, packing my things. I turned on the television and saw what at first I took to be a film. But as I continued to watch, I realized that it was not fiction but news. I stared as one – and then the other – of the twin towers of New York's World Trade Center collapsed. And then I *smiled*. Yes, despicable as it may sound, my initial reaction was to be remarkably pleased.
>
> Your disgust is evident; indeed, your large hand has, perhaps without your noticing, clenched into a fist. But please believe me when I tell you that I am

no sociopath; I am not indifferent to the suffering of others. When I hear of an acquaintance who has been diagnosed with a serious illness, I feel – almost without fail – a sympathetic pain, a twinge in my kidneys strong enough to elicit a wince. When I am approached for a donation to charity, I tend to be forthcoming, at least insofar as my modest means will permit. So when I tell you I was pleased at the slaughter of thousands of innocents, I do so with a profound sense of perplexity.

But at that moment, my thoughts were not with the victims of the attack – death on television moves me most when it is fictitious and happens to characters with whom I have built up relationships over multiple episodes – no, I was caught up in the *symbolism* of it all, the fact that someone had so visibly brought America to her knees. Ah, I see I am only compounding your displeasure. I understand, of course; it is hateful to hear another person gloat over one's county's misfortune. But surely you cannot be completely innocent of such feelings yourself. Do you feel no joy at the video clips – so prevalent these days – of American munitions laying waste the structures of your enemies?

But you are at war, you say? Yes, you have a point. I was not at war with America. Far from it, I was the product of an American university; I was earning a lucrative American salary; I was infatuated with an American woman. So why did part of me desire to see America harmed? I did not know then; I knew merely that my feelings would be unacceptable to my colleagues, and I undertook to hide them as well as I could. When my team gathered in Jim's room later that evening, I feigned the same shock and anguish I saw on the faces around me. (pp. 82–4)

At that moment when September 11th happens, Changez realizes that his relationship with America, with his work and his new life is more complicated than he thought. To get pleasure from what is so obviously a terrible thing suggests that there's something in him that needs to be pleased and that in fact is pleased by undermining the world that he is trying to build for himself. He tries to deny it and move beyond it, but like an echo it builds up in Changez and eventually takes him to the place where we find him at the beginning of the novel. But America is changing as well, the world is changing and a central theme in the novel is the notion of nostalgia. It is a natural thing, a human tendency to look back at the past with a kind of longing. I think it comes from the fact that we are all going to die, and so therefore, as we get older and death becomes closer, the time in our life when death was further away seems somehow charmed. When the world is changing rapidly and people are frightened, the impulse to look to that time before the fear grows stronger. Nostalgia becomes a very powerful thing. In this novel Erica of course is struck with a potentially fatal form of nostalgia in her love for the dead Chris. As Changez makes his way in America, he suffers from a kind of nostalgic attachment to this Pakistan that he can't really leave behind. And it seems to Changez that America itself is suddenly suffering from a kind of nostalgia; the America of the 1990s is giving way to the America where people are talking about honour and duty and wearing uniforms with lots of campaign medals on their chest. It is a very retro kind of thing, World War II America is manifesting itself and overtaking the anything-goes America of the Clinton years, dot.com boom, optimism, change. Instead we have a return to some kind of martial values, moral certitude, patriotism. And this strikes Changez as being deeply nostalgic. But his work is resolutely, remorselessly, inexorably forward looking – buying companies, restructuring them with no regard for the history of the people who work there or for the consequences for the community they work in. And he feels the contradiction as nostalgia starts to grip. But nostalgia of course is also played out in his love life with Erica. I now want to read a scene where Changez and Erica have sex:

> In my bed she asked me to put my arms around her, and I did so, speaking quietly in her ear. I knew she enjoyed my stories of Pakistan, so I rambled on about my family and Lahore. When I tried to kiss her, she did not move her lips or shut her eyes. So I shut them for her and asked, 'Are you missing Chris?' She nodded, and I saw tears begin to force themselves between her lashes. 'Then pretend,' I said, 'pretend I am him'. I do not know why I said it; I felt overcome and it seemed, suddenly, a possible way forward. 'What?' she said, but she did not open her eyes. 'Pretend I am him,' I said again. And slowly, in darkness and in silence, we did.
>
> I do not know how to describe my experience of what happened next; I cannot, of course, claim that I was possessed, but at the same time I did not seem to be myself. It was as though we were under a spell, transported to a world where I was Chris and she was with Chris, and we made love with a physical intimacy that Erica and I had never enjoyed. Her body denied mine no longer, I watched her shut eyes, and her shut eyes watched him.
>
> I can still recall her muscularity, made more pronounced by her gauntness, and the near-inanimate smoothness and coolness of her flesh as she leaned back and exposed to my touch her breasts. The entrance between her legs was wet and dilated, but was at the same time oddly rigid; it reminded me – unwillingly – of a wound, giving our sex a violent undertone despite the gentleness with which I attempted to move. More than once I smelled what I thought to be blood, but when I reached down to ascertain with my fingers whether it was her time of month, I found them unstained. She shuddered towards the end – grievously, almost mortally; her shuddering called forth my own.
>
> 'You're a kind person', she said afterwards, as we lay there. 'It sounds like a stupid thing to say but it's true.' I held her and did not reply. I felt something I have not felt before or since; I remember it well: I felt at once both *satiated* and *ashamed*. My satiation was understandable to me; my shame was more confusing. Perhaps by taking on the persona of another, I had diminished myself in my own eyes; perhaps I was humiliated by the continuing dominance, in the strange romantic triangle of which I found myself a part, of my dead rival; perhaps I was worried that I had acted selfishly and I sensed, even then, that I had done Erica some terrible harm. But this last explanation is – I hope – unlikely; surely I could not have known what would happen to her over the weeks and months to follow. (pp. 119–21)

And the last thing I will read today before we go over to questions is a little further on, towards the end of the novel. It takes place in Pakistan in the winter of 2001, at a time not dissimilar from now, as a terrorist attack had just taken place in India on the parliament in Delhi. The Indian government responded by mobilizing its armed forces on the Pakistani border and for a while it seemed that war was a possibility. Changez has gone back to Pakistan in December for his winter holidays and this is what he finds when he gets there:

> There are adjustments one must make if one comes here from America; a different way of observing is required. I recall the Americanness of my own gaze when I returned to Lahore that winter when war was in the offing. I was struck by how shabby our house appeared, with cracks running through its ceilings and dry bubbles of paint flaking off where dampness had entered its walls. The electricity had gone that afternoon, giving the place a gloomy air, but even in the dim light of the hissing gas heaters our furniture appeared dated and in urgent need of re-upholstery and repair. I was saddened to find it in such a state – no, more than saddened, I was ashamed. *This* was where I came from, this was my provenance, and it smacked of lowliness.
>
> But as I reacclimatized and my surroundings once again became familiar, it occurred to me that the house had not changed in my absence. I had changed; I was looking about me with the eyes of a foreigner, and not just any foreigner, but that particular type of entitled and unsympathetic foreigner who so annoyed me when I encountered him in the classrooms and workplaces of your country's elite. This realization angered me; staring at my reflection in the speckled glass of my bathroom mirror I resolved to exorcise the unwelcome sensibility by which I had become possessed.
>
> It was only after so doing that I saw my house properly again, appreciating its enduring grandeur, its unmistakable personality and idiosyncratic charm. Mughal miniatures and ancient carpets graced its reception rooms; an excellent library abutted its veranda. It was far from impoverished; indeed, it was rich with history. I wondered how I could ever have been so ungenerous – and so blind – to have thought otherwise, and I was disturbed by what this implied about myself: that I was a man lacking in substance and hence easily influenced by even a short sojourn in the company of others. (pp. 140–2)

And now I would like to invite your questions.

First questioner – Male: How were you challenged by writing this book?

MH: It took about seven years to write the book from inception to publication. I started writing it in the January before this September 11th happened. It was a fable about a Pakistani man working in corporate America who thinks he's a kind of Janissary. In the early draft, the book was mainly about that notion of being a Janissary, of being a servant in someone else's empire, one that was, whether intentionally or not, in effect functionally destroying one's own. I showed it to my agent in July 2001 and he said, 'You know, I don't really buy this Pakistani man, this Muslim guy living in New York, feeling really disenfranchised, wanting to go back.

Of course a few months later, he said, 'You know, that manuscript you were working on?...' But then September 11th had happened and my sort of quiet attempt to tell this story was overtaken by events. I spent some years continuing to write the novel set before September 11th. But I didn't know how to tell the story and not have the whole thing overwhelmed by September 11th. A novel set in New York that ends the summer of 2001 carries with it September 11th and it was impossible to escape that. As the years passed I no longer wanted to escape and I decided to set the novel within that event. [...], and then there was finding different ways of telling the story. I tried telling it as an American-accented first person ; I tried the third person; I tried all sorts of different things. I eventually came to this dramatic monologue where Changez is speaking to an American. For me it was personally very useful because, in the character of Changez, I got to imagine someone who contained within him certain impulses that I myself might have felt, which are of course only part of the complexity which is me. And out of these impulses, I fashioned a character and then set him into the world to walk a path, which is not a path that I'd walked. So in Changez I got to live a life as a 10 year-younger cousin of mine who, unlike me, hadn't lived half his life in America; unlike me, wasn't particularly prone to finding midpoints, and experienced events and their consequences in such a way. The useful thing for me is, having written that story, that my relationship to the things that I talk about changed. Oddly, I felt much more comfortable with the United States, with my position between Pakistan and India, between Pakistan and America, between America and Britain, all these different places that were in conflict. It may not be quite right to describe the book as an exorcism, but there is something of that, exploring a world through which I could have passed. I don't want to exaggerate the autobiographical aspects, though, [...] but living inside this character of Changez, who isn't me, to create it was very useful, because there was really an enormous amount of confusion, anger and tension, all sorts of things that the novel helped me explore.

Second questioner – Male: This will partly be a personal comment. I'm American, and when I read the novel, I thought the American is being pinned down; everything he does is observed, described, explained, [...] by Changez. At the end of the novel Changez suspects that the American is carrying a gun and the American suspects that he is being pursued by people with malicious intent, but Changez knows the situation, he knows how the American is going to react, and I felt a little bit paranoid at the end of this intensely detailed description. OK, Americans need to feel exposed as they are so busy showing the rest of the world how they should be. But my first reaction was anger. But when *you* read, I hear Changez as a much more tentative, self-reflective man, and in the novel I didn't hear that at all. I heard somebody who knew he was playing with somebody who was off his turf and who could be played with and whose own tendency towards action and violence could be exploited against him. In other words, the American felt trapped in ways presumably the American makes others feel trapped. In part my comment leads to asking how we can get reality to overcome the paranoid structures which are there and for which reality provides an outlet? In the novel there is no such outlet. I also wonder how the love scene fits in: it has a sort of oedipal structure to it, with Changez being in the position of the oedipal son since he is claiming the dead lover's position. Idealization would make the relationship with Erica impossible. And that was the one thing that I was really sad about. And one final point, the impossibility of that relationship fits in for me with how it all ended because it seems to me you left us in a paranoid position – that the emotional playing with the American's capacity for over-reaction was going to lead to trouble.

MH: This is interesting. I am very pleased that you reacted in the way that you did to the novel. Taking your first point about your initial reaction of anger, and the idea that the American is pinned down, I would say that this is done in the reverse way in which the media in the US particularly, but also in the UK around the time of September 11th, ascribed meaning to these faceless people out there. Who knows if this guy is right about what he is saying about this American? – We have no idea. But your response of anger is very interesting and the reason why I say I am pleased is because of the way I think that novels work. One of the interesting things about them as an art form (the least popular among the narrative forms compared to film or television) is, while they don't really have the power of reach, what they do have is a way of involving the audience to a great degree. When you read a novel, you are holding pulped wood, and looking at black squiggles of ink and the process of taking that and making that into a story hugely involves you, the reader. That co-creative aspect of reading a book is what is unique about books, particularly the kind of book which I think this attempts to be, one which maximizes the space for co-creation. There is a lot of open space for the audience to fill in and that is how interesting things happen; so the voice of Changez that you heard when you read it to yourself and the voice of Changez that you heard just now weren't the same. When you read *this* book, you are at least partly reading yourself, and that's why I think that your response, the anger that you felt was wonderful for me. There isn't only one way to read this. And it also depends on whether you think the novel is functioning straight. Isn't Changez just having a conversation with himself, with no American there? We may have here a man who has just gone nuts. I think you are right, the novel is manipulative but it declares its manipulative intent. It is manipulative less in the sense of someone commanding an invading army and more in the sense of someone asking you to dance. When you have a dance partner, you agree that a manipulation is taking place, but you are moving together, it's a mutual process, an interesting manipulation to engage in. It took me so long to answer that I feel like I might be blanking out on the second and third points – what were the second and third points?

Second questioner: It was about the love story and fantasy. The idealization of the ex-boyfriend into which Changez can't fit has to do with fantasy, and it obviously has an oedipal structure. The third point was about the sadness of it. Even though I agree with everything you are saying about the manipulation being more like a dance than an advancing army and that it gave me a chance to think about my projections, I still felt it was sad, because the failure of the relationship was also matched by what happened at end, how the novel was left.

MH: I will take the second point about Oedipus. As an author, I have only been to one other forum with psycho-anything in the title. It was a South Asian psychoanalytic, or psychiatric forum, I forget which, after my first novel *Moth Smoke* came out. A South Asian member of the psychology profession told me something very interesting. He said that the recurring myth of this inter-generational oedipal story plays itself out differently in South Asia, where very often it's not the case of the son desiring to destroy the father to sleep with the mother but rather it's the story of the father mistakenly thinking the son is a rival and destroying the son. And out of that comes something very interesting in the temporal sense. On a very simple, or simplistic level, it's the difference between the present attempting to destroy the past in Greece, and the past attempting to destroy the present in India. But that dynamic is interesting, because it shows how, in this relationship, the defeated party is really Changez. To the extent that there is a possibility of victory in this impossible love triangle, the victory is Chris's. I agree with you that this is sad: the victory of the past over the future does feel sad. It is also about the feeling of nostalgia that I was talking about earlier, about the past pressing on the present. In political terms, whether it's an Osama bin Laden-type claim that we should return to something modelled on a thousand year-old Caliphate, or a George Bush-type claim that we should return to the generation that fought World War II, these are all claims that are nostalgic and are manifestations of the past trying to destroy the present. To try to imagine what a future could be that isn't desperately nostalgic is the great political challenge that I see for this time and it is the reason why the novel ends on a sad note (I think you are right, there). But embedded in that is also the possibility that, when Changez goes on television and makes these kinds of anti-American statements picked up on networks and carried internationally, he is secretly hoping that a disappeared Erica might see it and somehow respond. Embedded in that hope is a possible alternate motivation for him and another possible ending or direction for the novel to take, once the American and Changez part ways. Certainly, as a person, this is something I am much more excited to see happening, the resumption of some kind of a relationship and the creation of a future. So there is sadness, I agree, but hopefully not unmitigated sadness.

Third questioner – Female: I was very interested in that last exchange because I realize I had read the end of the novel very differently. I thought that Changez was incredibly naïve and that the person he was talking to throughout the novel was the person who was sent to assassinate him. And so I was intrigued by the idea of assassination as a way of representing America on the last page. I was fascinated when you said that it is not even clear whether America was there at all.

But my question was really about Erica. I come from a long tradition of feminist literary criticism which is very suspicious of mad women in literature, especially when it's mad girls in books written by boys. You could say that the political dilemma of Changez as Janissary and as being in America post-9/11 gets offloaded onto Erica's pathology. The body of the woman then carries the political disenchantment of the main character; it carries a very grave burden and something about that makes me feel very uncomfortable, in that it just joins a long trope of what we used to call 'the mad woman in the attic'.

MH: I think that is very fair. For a rather different female character, you should check out *Moth Smoke*. But to take your second point first: absolutely! Erica is very much of this mad-woman-by-guys school of writing. All I would offer as an explanation is that it is a sort of 'mad people' book. Changez (in my measure) is no less mad than Erica actually. And also, in the novel I tried to make clear the possibility that Changez has clearly misunderstood what Erica's story is. So that when he reads her novella, he doesn't see anything of her in it. When she disappears and he can't find her, it does occur to him that she may have another story of which he is not a part, and she is sort of resolutely insisting throughout the novel that there is this Erica narrative which is not given to this book to tell. In fact he recognizes something of this when he still tries to reach out for her; there is in the novel the sense that Erica may still exist. So I think that Erica's madness and fate should be read very carefully through the lens of Changez's madness and fate. Should you really believe that his tale of Erica and Erica's tale of Erica would be the same thing? Obviously not, it may be that they would be drastically opposed. Erica is portrayed as a mad woman scorned, and in that sense you are right to feel uncomfortable. But the American is portrayed as a belligerent, crew-cut killer and the Muslim is portrayed as a fundamentalist, in the school of clever Eastern, murderous characters. But my intention was to create very recognizable types and subvert them along the way. Whether the subversion of Erica's type is successful or not is something that is up to every reader to decide and certainly something that I was setting out to do. The sex scene between them sort of ties back to what was said earlier about a certain notion of fundamentalism, in that there is something of a tragically perverted romance at the core. In other words, I think of somebody who flies an aircraft into a building as – this is probably the right literary comparison here – a kind of knight errant. At least that would be part of the self-perception involved. In other words, somebody who has set out to kill dragons, somebody who has this enormous romantic quest. I haven't thought through necessarily how or what that means, but for me it is something that lies at the heart of fundamentalism, this notion of the perverted romantic quest, that is certainly found within the character of Changez and this call towards terrorism, which he may or may not follow. Many young men (I'm not talking now about people who have actually seen a loved one killed or have some direct revenge motive), many young people have this sense of vague societal wrong which in their minds seems to link up with this world-conquering impulse that we can see throughout history and throughout literature – you know: climbing the mountain, slaying the dragon, doing a great heroic deed. That line of thought led me to want to explore a sexual relationship that had that kind of element to it, a romantic quest, like Romeo and Juliet, a person who would die for their love. But on closer inspection, this pure romantic quest appears sick and somehow wrong. That is how I wound up in that space.

Fourth questioner – Male: I am interested in this notion of I/am/ America. Are you trying to demonstrate how Man and America can come together and therefore there's hope for the future or are you trying to demonstrate that Man and America are inevitably split and divided and there's no hope for the future?

MH: I'm trying to create a Petri dish in which organisms interested in that question can flourish. But this issue of names is very much there – you know Erica, and Changez's perception of her as victim of this destructive nostalgia, is one side of it, as you say I/am/America. And Underwood Samson, the company he works for with the initials U.S. is a remorselessly forward-looking meritocratic, transformative, outward-looking, future-orientated America. Both are playing themselves out in the novel and, if you ask me as a person how I would think about what you have just said, my answer is America is 300 million different people and, when we look at a constellation like that as a whole and not as a cluster of tiny components, we are already beginning to drift into dangerous territory. So I don't mean to posit either Erica or Underwood Sampson as America, only that they can be read as some notion of America and the reason why it is difficult for me to say, or for the novel to say, that this is how it pronounces on things, is because I really do believe that it is at least in part the job of the novelist to re-complicate what has been over-simplified. That is very much what I'm trying to do. And so: is Jim gay? Does Erica kill herself? Is Erica actually fine at the end of the book? Is the American there to kill him? Is he there to kill the American? On close inspection, there is no certain answer to any of those questions or to a lot of other questions in the book. This is intentional, not because I myself want to be evasive about what I think, but because I wanted the novel to be a kind of antidote to the certainty that was being bandied about so disastrously in the first few years of this century.

Questioner five – Male: This reminds me of the discussion in the previous session about Islam being multiple. In a similar way, Changez and America are multiple.

MH: That point of the multiple is hugely important because the one thing about the novel that nobody ever comments on is that just as Erica may be a suicidal woman who doesn't commit suicide and the American in the novel is the potential killer who may just be a tourist, there is also the point that, as best we can tell from this novel, there is no evidence whatsoever that Changez is religious beyond the fact that when he gets his job at Underwood Sampson he says spontaneously, 'Thank you god!' And so how he stands for some notion of Islam is very interesting to me. So many of the reviews and discussions of this book have been about that. But Changez is a secular humanist really, with a kind of tribal nationalism that attaches itself to Muslims. What that makes him in terms of religion is very much open to debate. I think that the notion of setting up a representative of Islam who is arguably not a Muslim or spiritually not a Muslim was something that I was playing with as well.

Questioner six – Female: I am assuming that you speak another language, so my question is: do you think in English? And my second question is: the name Changez, does it have a meaning?

MH: I speak Urdu as well as English and I mangle Italian from time to time and I speak different Englishes. Having lived in the UK for a while I speak a different English from having lived a dozen years or so in America. When I go to Pakistan and talk to my friends my English changes. This novel is written in a very different voice from my first; even in the drafts, there were so many different ones. I tend to think in my Englishes mostly and sometimes in my Urdus and, when I am in Pakistan in a more Urdu-speaking world, the Urdu does come back more. In my household more English is spoken than Urdu. I went to schools where, among eight subjects a day, only two would be taught in Urdu, so my language has been more English from the beginning.

As far as Changez is concerned: somebody pointed this out to me, they said that his name is changes and he changes and I said, 'Oh my god, I never thought of that', which is true. My French translator said, 'I think it is a bit heavy-handed for him to be named *Changez*, we're going to call him Tchenguiz, T.C.H.E.N.G.U.I.Z', and I said, 'That's so cool', if only

I had thought of that myself I would have changed it to Tchenguiz in all the languages. But to come back to the point of this non-Muslim, Muslim character, the historical figure of Changez is an Urdu name for Genghis, in the same way as Sikander is Alexander. Genghis's role of course in south-west Asian history, that of the famous Genghis anyway, is of the invader who attacks and destroys the Caliphate, the largest and most successful Muslim empire of its time. So Changez is paradoxically a kind of warrior figure who is counter Muslim. That notion interested me in creating this character because when he works in the corporate world there is a certain warrior aspect to him, there is a sort of martial overtone in the way he thinks about life. He does see himself, to a certain extent, as a sort of warrior. The audience is encouraged in seeing him as a warrior. But on whose behalf? That is not really answered. For people who are familiar with Muslim history, the Changez name is a warning not to read this character as his appearance would suggest. He has a beard and he is Pakistani, but don't assume he stands for Muslims, because his name implies the opposite.

Thank you.

Reference

Hamid, M. (2007) *The Reluctant Fundamentalist*. London, New York, NY: Penguin Books.

ABSTRACT

The author reads from, discusses and responds to questions about his novel *The Reluctant Fundamentalist*, a narrative concerning the psychological consequences of the events of 9/11 for a young Pakistani man working in corporate America. Themes of nostalgia, alienation and distrust are explored, as well as the role that literature can play in sustaining ambivalence.

Key words: capitalism, fundamentalism, literature, nostalgia

DOI: 10.3366/E1460823509000427

RETREAT FROM REALITY

David Modell, London, UK

Andrea Williams fell in love with Jesus at the age of 4. 'I was put on a bus to go to Sunday school,' she says, 'one of the teachers told me all about Jesus and really I fell in love with him there and then, and it hasn't changed since.' That relationship with Jesus has now all but taken over her life. We are on our way to an anti-abortion rally in London, where Andrea will address the crowd and tell them that abortion is a 'silent holocaust' and that we must 'repent' in order to change the nation.

On the way we make a brief stop at a Christian book-shop. After a few minutes Andrea emerges with a weighty plastic bag. In it are several books she has bought for me; it appears they are intended to aid my conversion.

Andrea is the Public Policy Director of the Lawyers Christian Fellowship. I am spending time with her for a documentary I am making for Channel 4 about Christian Fundamentalists. The Christians are the latest subject group in a series of programmes I have made over several years about extremists.

Outside Parliament there are a few hundred people. Andrea has brought the placards and starts to hand them out enthusiastically. She is the principal organizer of the protest and one of the key figures in the anti-abortion movement (see Fig. 1). Watching her buzz around marshalling the demonstrators, I'm tempted to describe her as being possessed by a messianic fervour.

But this is when Andrea is at her happiest, fighting the good fight. Doing what she can to save the nation, to transform it, because it seems we are descending into the clutches of unimaginable evil. Andrea later tells me: 'There's a spiritual battle going on today.' She believes liberal legislation is 'a rejection of God and any rejection of God is the work of God's enemy, Satan'.

At times Andrea reminds me of the animal rights activists who were the subject of a previous film. Like them she finds the real world almost intolerable; she sees evidence of Satan's work everywhere (homosexuality,

---

DAVID MODELL is a filmmaker and writer who has made a number of important documentaries about contemporary racism, Nazism and Christian fundamentalism in the UK. Address for correspondence: David Modell, c/o Bonakdar Cleary, 35 Charles Square, London N1 6HT. [david@davidmodell.com]

Figure 1. **Andrea Williams on an anti-abortion rally in London, 2007**
© David Modell

the worship of other faiths, the 'silent holocaust' of abortion). She finds comfort in an alternative utopian idea – an idealized society that she carries with her inside her head. For her, that imagined world is one where everyone shares her strict Christian beliefs and our laws restrain 'unchristian' behaviour.

For the animal rights extremists, the objections to the real world are even more visceral. Again, the word 'holocaust' is used to describe what is happening around them. Their central philosophy, that all life is of equal value, means that evidence of our murderous relationship with animals is everywhere. Farms become concentration camps. Their utopian alternative is a world in which all animals are truly liberated. Where human beings no longer have the right to subjugate their fellow animals or use them for any purpose whatsoever.

It is no surprise that Andrea is at her happiest on the barricades outside parliament. For many fundamentalists, existing in the real world is easiest when fighting to replace it with their imagined alternative. Activism not only brings relief, for some it is essential for survival. Mel Broughton (see Fig. 2) runs a campaign against the building of an animal experimentation laboratory in Oxford. A long-time member of the Animal Liberation Front he is currently awaiting trial for a suspected firebombing.

Mel was one of the principal contributors in a documentary I made in 2006. He is in his early 40s and lives alone in a bed-sit with his dog Bella. He has totally dedicated his life to the cause. During an interview he suddenly lurches forward and grabs Bella by the collar. It seems she was about to try

Figure 2. **Mel Broughton [© David Modell]**

and eat a wasp making its way slowly across the carpet. Mel tenderly picks up the insect on a piece of card and places it gently on the window ledge. I ask him if he's going to put it out. 'No,' he replies 'it's a bit cold outside, so I'm helping it.'

It may be tempting to laugh at this apparently irrational behaviour, but Mel is deadly serious. Later in the interview he spells out the torment he carries with him and how he copes with it: 'I'll pass cattle trucks on the way to slaughter, I'll walk down the road and pass a butchers, there's no getting away from it, it's a constant thing to deal with. It's just all there in your head, all the time. The only way I can deal with it is to fight and keep fighting. I either stand up and fight or I go under.'

At the heart of all fundamentalist thinking is a central 'truth'. For Mel it is the truth that all animal life (including human) is of equal value. For Andrea it is The Truth as spelled out in contemporary versions of the Old Testament. For neo-Nazis it is that the 'white race' (however they might define it) is superior to all others and should therefore have dominion over them.

Knowing these truths not only puts the believer at odds with society, it also provides them with a sense of absolute moral certainty and an ethical code which permits outlandish and often provocative behaviour. Mel believes his moral code trumps that of the society in which he finds himself; he therefore feels justified in having carried out past quasi-terrorist offences.

Figure 3. **Stephen Green [© David Modell]**

Andrea might be working within the law to change our laws, but she is willing to express such hostile views about other people (homosexuals, Muslims) that she gets very close to inciting hatred. In defence she will say she has a duty to 'speak The Truth'; that is after all what Jesus did, despite the fact that some found it offensive.

Crucially, that 'truth' is absolute. It cannot therefore be influenced by inconvenient evidence to the contrary. Which puts Andrea in an interesting position because, as a trained barrister, part of her campaign against godless legislation is fought in the courts.

While I'm filming with her, she's trying to sabotage some gay rights legislation in an employment tribunal and cites questionable evidence about developmental outcomes for children brought up in gay households. She later tells me: 'It's amazing, the evidence always comes out in favour of a biblical interpretation of life.' So I ask her how old she believes the world is. 'About 4000 years' is her reply. I suggest that there is not a lot of evidence to support that, but quite a lot to support the idea that it is several billion years older. There is a pause, and then it appears she's unable to answer. In the end, she holds firm to her belief; no amount of opposing evidence will influence her.

Stephen Green (see Fig. 3) is a friend of Andrea's and prefers an even more 'direct-action' approach to transform society. He runs a small organization called Christian Voice, a protest group that was instrumental

Figure 4. **Mark Collett [© David Modell]**

in the successful campaign to close down *Gerry Springer the Opera*. Like
Andrea he is at his happiest when carrying out what he interprets as God's
work.

He clearly delights in picketing gay events and festivals, handing out
anti-homosexual literature and trying to provoke confrontation. While I'm
filming him outside 'Gay Sunday' at London Zoo, a woman is so offended
by him she tells me he is carrying out a 'hate crime'. Because he knows 'The
Truth' Stephen can justify his offensive behaviour. God has issued him with
a licence to provoke.

The need to provoke anger in others is a recurring theme among the
extremists I have spent time with. My first study of fundamentalism was
in 2002. I spent much of that year following Mark Collett, then leader of the
Young British National Party (see Fig. 4). A 22 year-old university student,
he challenged the stereotype of the street-fighting neo-Nazi.

At a time when the BNP were trying to appear more mainstream,
I followed a besuited Mark around deprived estates in Yorkshire, knocking
on doors and sounding every bit the young politician. It wasn't until the
night of the local elections that I got a different insight into his personality.

Mark had stood for election as a councillor (and lost badly) and the Anti-
Nazi League had mounted a demonstration outside the town hall. As Mark
emerged after the count, about 100 protesters surrounded him and his small
entourage and began yelling: 'Nazi scum, get off our streets.' Mark raised

Figure 5. **John Pearce [© David Modell]**

his arms in delight and stuck out his chin in what surely must have been an attempt to emulate Mussolini; he looked every bit the young Fascist and was revelling in the attention. The van that should have arrived to take Mark and his group away was held up; he was on the receiving end of a huge amount of raw fury, but I'd never seen him look happier.

The attraction of a narrow, inflexible belief system isn't merely that it permits certain behaviour. It is also a powerful tool of personal restraint. My travels among the Christian fundamentalists started with an encounter at a demonstration (organized by Andrea) against gay rights legislation. I was all but accosted by a young man called John Pearce (see Fig. 5), holding a placard that read: 'Homosexuality is an abomination – Jesus is the only way'.

A few weeks later, I visit John's church in Bristol and spend the day with him. After lunch we go to do an interview in his shared flat. He shows me into his room, and I immediately notice a large piece of paper taped to the ceiling directly above his bed. In large black letters is the word 'Jesus'. 'What's that?' I ask, and John explains: 'Sometimes when you wake up in the morning all these thoughts start coming into your mind and when I look at that I realize that's where my focus needs to be, on Him.' Unsurprisingly, those unwelcome thoughts are often sexual. At 29, John is still a virgin.

The devotion to his belief is as strong as that of any others I've met in different fundamentalist movements. Like them, that obvious commitment to the cause brings rewards within the group. John's church, Carmel Christian Centre, is far more than simply a place of worship. They run a faith school (which teaches creationism as scientific fact), a bible college and various community 'outreach' programmes, all with the aim of winning converts. John has become a 'church leader' with responsibility for educating the young people, and also teaches in the bible college. He has achieved a sense of status, found a welcoming community and feels valued and important.

Much the same could be said of Mark Collett. The BNP saw him as a valuable asset and at the time were marking him out as a future leader. Not only did he have status, being an important part of the BNP made him feel powerful. So much so that it was only when he was outside that context, standing for a class photo with his university peers, that I saw him as he might have been feeling most of the time: lost and inadequate.

All these groups bind themselves together with a fierce adherence to a narrow belief system. Within the group their world-view is constantly reaffirmed and never challenged. A key component to the way they function is the recruitment of converts so the belief can be propagated – thus making it more 'real'. If someone outside the group can be convinced of your belief, then that must make it true. I'm sure that part of the reason the different movements have engaged with me is because they see it as an opportunity to convert me to the cause and see that reflected in a TV programme which will validate their beliefs.

If we accept that the membership share an idea of an alternative, internal society, then it is not surprising that these groups become manifestations of that alternative society. Apparently rejecting of and isolated from the rest of us, it becomes easy to view them as 'cults'.

As I've been making these films I have been intrigued by the question of whether the people I have spent time with see the world as they do because of the causes they have found, or whether the cause was found because of a pre-existing need.

It is difficult to be conclusive, but certainly for many there does seem to be evidence of an earlier disturbance which could explain why a particular fundamentalist belief works for them. Typically, John from Carmel might be quickly identified as being in retreat from his own homosexual tendencies and that his belief gives him the power to abstain from something terrifying. But I would suggest that's too simplistic.

During the filming John acquired a fiancée and prepared to move to a matrimonial home. His parents (both evangelical Christians) came to help him decorate and were keen (on camera) to discuss homosexuality; his mum was forthright in expressing her total disgust for such practices. During our conversation, however, John's dad disclosed that he had had 'homosexual urges' and even perhaps the occasional experience. He went on to say, somewhat sadly, that he used his faith to control himself.

This made me wonder if John had grown up in an environment where homosexuality might have been seen as a threat to the survival of the family. Or perhaps sex more broadly was seen as something powerful and dangerous that needed to be controlled. Against this background, the fact that he chose to adhere to a belief system (already around him in the family) that imposed sexual abstinence does not seem very surprising.

It was among the Animal Rights Activists that I found the strongest connections with earlier experiences. Mel Broughton talked about feeling depressed as an adolescent and that he was 'looking for something'. He knew he was getting close to it when he joined a group of hunt saboteurs, but only felt he had really found it when he joined the ALF (Animal Liberation Front). But it was another activist, a young woman called Gail Record, whose thinking I could best understand.

Gail was born with a curvature of the spine, an acute condition that caused her upper body to become compressed, putting stress on her major organs. As a young girl she had treatment to try and correct the condition; this treatment was not terribly sophisticated. From the ages of 12 to 14 Gail spent many months in hospital. Bolts were screwed into her forehead and her entire body was placed on a metal rack, in order to stretch her. She had to remain like this, virtually paralysed for weeks on end. The treatment was so stressful that she almost died.

Gail has a memory of being wheeled into the grounds of the hospital where she could watch the animals in an adjacent field. She says that next to the hospital was a medical research establishment and these animals carried obvious wounds from experimental operations. She says she knew how those animals were feeling.

Gail's mother is also an ardent supporter of the animal liberation cause. Like many in the movement, their principal focus is on the vivisection industry. While we are having tea in her kitchen Gail's mum tells me that, if she were to be diagnosed with a terminal illness, she would delight in suicide bombing a well-known animal research company. I later join Gail and her mum (see Fig. 6) on a demonstration at a site in Oxford where an animal research lab is being built. Gail has brought her favourite protest banner with her – it's an enormous picture of a monkey fixed to a metal rack with bolts in its forehead.

On the picket line, Gail's mum is simply terrifying as she shouts at the builders: 'Your children will have to live with this, the murder, the torture, the hate. Ahhh, are you frightened?' Gail joins in: 'Can you imagine what it's like to have bolts screwed into your head? Not being able to move? Can you imagine the pain with no pain relief?'

Later Gail tells me: 'I can identify with the monkey in the picture. It's very painful – and to keep those bolts in place they have to tighten them once a week. And they don't use anaesthetic; you just go crunch, crunch, crunch. And you can literally hear your skull grinding, feel it grinding.' Her mum

Figure 6. **Gail Record and her mother Joan [© David Modell]**

then adds: 'I can remember when Gail first had it done; I fainted nine times before I could even look at her. When you're watching them each week with their screwdrivers tightening up the nuts and bolts, you've never seen anyone suffer so much.' She then finishes with a chilling glare: 'What goes around comes around.'

Gail's treatment must have felt and looked like torture. For both her and her mother. In the monkey, they saw Gail's suffering. It was as if the scientists and the builders of the lab had become responsible for what Gail went through and therefore, for Gail and her mum, they had become legitimate targets for their residual anger.

It is not known if the procedure depicted in the photo of the monkey is going to be repeated within the walls of the lab in Oxford, but for the protestors that's not strictly relevant. That image is one of several regularly used by the activists to represent the horror of vivisection. To them, these laboratories are places of torture and extermination. Described again as concentration camps.

I am sure that for many like Gail and her mother the buildings are little more than convenient places to project their own internal torment, a focus for their own suffering and anger; but there was something else striking about the lab in Oxford, which I believe is representative of the way governments respond to perceived threats from extremists.

The activists at Oxford were dedicated and well organized, but there were not many of them. The offences committed in the campaign against the lab were very unpleasant but rarely involved a threat to life. Nonetheless, the government seemed determined to see them as terrorists and (after the first

Figure 7. **Workers at an animal research lab in Oxford [© David Modell]**

group of contractors pulled out, citing intimidation) took over the building of the lab in what could fairly be described as a military operation.

An enormous floodlit barrier was erected around the site, topped with razor wire and security cameras. Private security guards and police with powers to stop and search anyone in the vicinity patrolled the perimeter. The security personnel and all the builders on site were instructed to wear balaclavas in order to protect them from being identified by the protestors (see Fig. 7). All vehicles entering and leaving were painted grey to anonymize them fully.

The surreal effect was to create something that exactly matched the protestors' fantasies. Every day they saw their view of the world reinforced by the behaviour of the state; therefore their own behaviour was legitimized. The government had responded as states often do: a response which is in itself more extreme than the threat posed by the extremists, as though unable to resist the provocation.

Fundamentalists exist in and pose challenges to all societies, and their presence must be taken seriously. But simplistic responses risk simply validating their arguments and creating the conditions in which extremism can grow. Perhaps the key is to demonstrate that, on balance, reality is a better place to exist in than any imagined alternative.

References

Modell, D. (2002) *Young, Nazi and Proud*. Channel 4 TV.
Modell, D. (2006) *Mad About Animals*. Channel 4 TV.
Modell, D. (2008) *In God's Name*. Channel 4 TV.

ABSTRACT

Drawing on the author's experience of making a number of television documentaries for about extremism, this paper attempts to explore the commonalities between different groups who pursue extremist or fundamentalist ideals. The intention is to develop a better understanding of those who are drawn towards fundamentalism, whether they be animal rights activists, racial supremacists or religious extremists.

Key words: Christian fundamentalism, animal rights, BNP

DOI: 10.3366/E1460823509000439

HUMANITY AND ITS GODS: ATHEISM[1]

Elisabeth Roudinesco, Paris, France

To approach our general theme of fundamentalism, I have decided to invoke for you a certain kind of materialism that I consider to be my own, the materialism of Enlightenment philosophy and of Darwinism; but also the need for the divine within the human, as a counterpoint to man's capacity for crime, for violence or abjection. I will speak of the gods of Ancient Greece, and of heroes, that is to say those demi-gods capable of giving their life for the *polis*, accepting the 'good death', like Achilles, for example. Finally, I will also touch on monotheism, the three religions of the Book, Judaism, Christianity and Islam, of which I am only familiar with the first two.

I will start by telling you about my personal journey through classical culture and the two kinds of monotheism that have left their mark on me.

Christians consider me to be a Christian since I have been baptised, received communion and been brought up within the Catholic religion. I do mean religion rather than faith, although I have to say that I cannot define myself as a 'Christian'. I am not really such: I have no faith; I haven't even lost it since I have never possessed it. Moreover, subjectively, I do not feel myself to be a Christian.

But, on the other hand, I am also not at all certain of being Jewish although, in the eyes of many Jews, I would appear a Jew, not by adhering to Judaism, but through 'identity' or 'belonging'. Whether I like it or not, I am part of that very particular people, the 'Godless Jews', to whom

---

1. Translated from the French by Julia Borossa.

ELISABETH ROUDINESCO is Professor and Head of Research in the Department of History at the University of Paris VII – Denis Diderot and President of the International Society of the History of Psychiatry and Psychoanalysis. She is the author of around 20 books, numerous articles and collaborative works, translated into 30 languages. In particular: *Jacques Lacan & Co.: A History of Psychoanalysis in France, 1925–1985* (Chicago University Press, 1990); *Madness and Revolution: The Lives and Legends of Theroigne De Mericourt* (Verso, 1993); *Jacques Lacan* (Columbia University Press, 1999); *Why Psychoanalysis?* (*European Perspectives: A Series in Social Thought and Cultural Criticism*, Columbia University Press, 2003); *For What Tomorrow . . . : A Dialogue with Jacques Derrida* (Stanford University Press, 2004). Address for correspondence: 89 avenue Denfert-Rochereau, 74014 Paris, France.

the term '*judéité* – Jewishness' has been assigned, understood as a way of feeling Jewish, independently from Judaism, a way of continuing to think oneself as Jewish in the modern world whilst being materialist, humanist or atheist. From that point of view, yes, I do feel Jewish. This kind of split between a religion and a genealogy only exists in the history of the Jews and does not seem to be present in the other monotheisms. Christianity, for example, does not imply a particular identity. Instead, one talks of 'Christian culture' to describe how a subject may have been brought up within the Christian religion. And that absence of an implied identity means that the significance of the phrase 'Christian culture' is therefore not the same as that of Jewishness which means much more than a cultural tradition.

A story recounted by Gershom Scholem illustrates what is entailed in this identity, defined by an inheritance or rather by a 'remainder':

> When the Baal Schem Tov had a difficult task to accomplish, he would go to a certain place in the forest, light a fire and say a silent prayer; and what he needed to accomplish was resolved. When a generation later, the Maggid of Meseritz found himself faced with the task, he went to the same place in the forest and said: 'We no longer know how to light the fire, but we still know how to say the prayer'. And what he needed to accomplish was resolved. A generation later, Rabbi Moshe Leib de Sassov had the same task to accomplish. He too went to the forest and said: 'We no longer know how to light the fire, we no longer know the mysteries of the prayer, but we still know the exact place in the forest where it all used to take place, and that should be enough'. And it was enough. But when another generation passed and the Rabbi Israel de Rishin was faced with the task, he stayed in his house sitting in his armchair and said: 'We no longer know how to light the fire, we don't know how to say the prayers, we don't even know the place in the forest, but we still know how to tell the story'. And the story he told had the same effect as the practices of his predecessors. (Scholem 1973, p. 368)

This story of 'remainders' attests to a specificity that derives from the very nature of Judaism, a religion of belonging founded on the idea of a transmission or of an alliance, on a cult of memory, an obedience to ancestral rites, be they repressed, refused or avoided, rather than on free will (as in Protestantism) or on the knowledge of God and an adherence to an institution (the Catholic Church).

My father was Jewish, certainly, but had no God or religion, though he was circumcised. He led a secular life, and was brought up in Romania not within the (Christian) Orthodox religion, but *with* the Orthodox religion, which allowed Romanian Jews to bypass their Jewishness in a country which was particularly anti-Semitic.

By emigrating to France, ten years after the Dreyfus affair, he followed the path of assimilation, whereby Jews occluded their Jewishness and proclaimed their support for the Republic, for the homeland of human rights. A patriot, my father enrolled voluntarily in 1914 into the French army so as to fight the Germans. Later, he considered himself a 'catholic', not for his love of the religion, but for his love of Renaissance art – Leonardo and Michelangelo.

My mother was Jewish through her mother, who saw herself as an 'Israelite' and was a supporter of the French Republic, secular and pro-Dreyfus, quite distinct from the Jewish immigrants from the East, whom she regarded with contempt, thereby marking out her dislike of all religion, to the point of anti-clericalism and anti-Catholicism.

But my mother was also connected to the Reformation church through her own father who belonged to Protestant High Society. Even though my grandfather had married an 'Israelite', he had no sympathy for Jews, and felt humiliated by being very much less intelligent than his wife, who in turn held him in contempt for his conservative ideas. In her youth, my mother had attended the Protestant Church.

Therefore, I was brought up without *religion* but with a very strong presence of *religions* in my life: in terms of a culture, a tradition, an identity, a story, a memory. This in turn connected me to three great paradigms: the intellect, desire, freedom.

The Jewishness of my father, together with the 'Israelism' of my maternal grandmother, represented the values of *logos*. And with this, I felt myself connected to the tradition of the book. From a very young age, I wanted to become a writer, which was a way of wanting to be Jewish through an elitist choice: I wanted to belong to the people of the intellectuals, from Voltaire to Hugo; they represented for me something like a chosen people.

If Jewishness for me represented reason and knowledge, Catholicism functioned as a connection to art, to desire, to sex, to sensuality – in other words, it allowed for the possibility of being in a state of permanent transgression. The painters that I admired through my father had taken hold of Catholic tradition in order to inscribe within their work an art of transgression. Just look at the bodies painted by Michelangelo on the wall of the Sistine Chapel dedicated to the Last Judgement and you will be convinced. Moreover, the practice of confession, the act of forgiveness, presupposes the commission of sin. As for Protestantism, inherited from my mother through the paternal branch of her family tree, it communicated itself through a strong attachment to the idea of free choice, to freedom, to a sense of individualism and a respect for science: an ethical and political commitment.

Thus it was through the visual arts that I gained access to the power of Roman Catholic religion. I became aware of it very early in my life, since, throughout my childhood, I was taken to the great museums of Europe. My father loved travelling and I was his companion on extremely cultural holidays, to Rome, for example. What I discovered in that city was not faith or the love of God, but beauty.

However, to escape from the power of the father, from the age of 9, I replaced this classical tradition with an art from my time whose content escaped the authority of the family: cinema, a space that enabled desire, transgression. This was a space where it was possible to become other than what one was; a space where it was possible to take on another identity.

I developed a passion for classical Hollywood cinema which has remained with me to this day. Between 1953 and 1963, I encountered the God of the Jews and of the Christians in Technicolor and in cinemascope through the great actors of the time: Robert Taylor, Richard Burton, Charlton Heston; *Quo Vadis?* (1951), *The Robe* (1953), *The Ten Commandments* (1956), and later *Ben Hur* (1959).

And so I became familiar with Christianity through the story of the first Roman century, where mad, bloodthirsty emperors opposed the martyrs of the faith. As for Judaism, I discovered it via its Christian representation, as recreated by Hollywood.

In fact, since American cinema was never very good at representing Greek antiquity, I only got to know the Gods of Mount Olympus (inherited by the Romans) by reading the *Iliad* and the *Odyssey*: stories of men, of gods, of heroes. The heroes in those books reminded me of the heroes of the Resistance. From June 1940, members of my family had taken part in the Resistance, in particular my mother and her brother; she, a leftist supporter of De Gaulle, later a socialist, a quasi-communist and he, like my father, a conservative, a right-wing supporter of De Gaulle. No member of my family ever wore the yellow star; none was deported, with the exception of a great-uncle who considered himself protected by his status of a Frenchman, a 'good *Israélite*'.

I saw the heroes of the Second World War in the guise of the heroes of Ancient Greece. I felt a particular sympathy for the Catholic priests involved in the Resistance, namely for a certain Abbé Bouvet, whom I had never met but whom I loved as a character from the films of Jean Renoir. With great generosity, he had forged birth certificates for my parents: I found them in their archives.

All this is to say that, even though I felt neither really Christian, nor really Jewish, I was convinced that I was the inheritor of a Judeo-Christian tradition, to which I had annexed the inheritance of Ancient Greece, its gods. I like these gods best, since they underwent constant metamorphosis and, in their struggle against one another, they never embodied the conflict between an absolute evil and a higher good. The gods of Greece could be everything at the same time, just like human beings in fact, one thing and its very opposite.

If Catholicism was thus the embodiment of desire, of art and of transgression, if Jewishness was the source of intellect, and if Protestantism connected me to free will or to the principles of morality, Greek culture functioned like a true ego ideal: to be a hero or not to be at all. To serve a cause higher than that of one's little ego, or the small difference of one's narcissism, or disappear.

I was therefore an atheist in its 18th-century sense, nourished by the double culture of Ancient Greece and Judeo-Christianity. Later, after May 1968, after that moment of transgressive joy that today's Versailles would like to see abolished, my education continued and I had the chance to meet the philosophers for whom I later wrote a book of farewells (Roudinesco 2008). I am referring particularly to Louis Althusser and Gilles Deleuze, to Jacques Derrida and Georges Canguilhem, whom I encountered later, but also to the one who really introduced me to history, Father Michel de Certeau. He was a Jesuit, an extraordinary one who compared Christian mysticism to psychoanalysis, emphasizing that both constituted a critique of the unity of the individual, of the privilege of consciousness and of the myth of progress (de Certeau 1982).

Marked by this teaching, I felt little sympathy for the militant atheism of the second half of the 20th century. I feared it gave expression to another kind of religion, not materialistic, but rather mechanistic, narcissistic, regressive: leading to the idea of the man machine with his neurones and with the sum of his behaviours. This is a kind of barbarism which champions the end of the human exception. Like all forms of reductionism, it also constitutes a great folly.

Of course, Deleuze had dreamed of this, as did La Mettrie in the 18th-century, but he did so in a playful way, outside the reaches of the State where the man machine finds its place today, supported by political regimes that only think in terms of measurement, appraisal, speculation.

Militant atheism seems to me as dangerous as other kinds of fundamentalist forms of servitude, as dangerous as the fetishized forms of expertise of the human. It places quantification and *jouissance* in the space of desire and returns to the very thing that it proposed to combat: the moral order, the imperative of servitude, the obedience to a dogma.

Furthermore, militant atheism tries to destroy secularism as much as religion, by making a parody of its ideals, substituting for them an authoritarian pedagogy.

There is no people without religion. Palaeontologists have shown that the establishment of *homo sapiens* depended on the invention of burial sites, in other words on a specifically human need to think beyond an organic body. This is the foundation of all religions. In fact, the invention of religion is accompanied by a capacity to represent dreams as much as reality. This is the source of art and of the capacity to create. The link to reproduction is there as well. Indeed the care of what lies beyond death is something that accompanies impregnation as well. On one side we have mourning and the homage to the dead, behold the sepulchre; on the other, consolation and the promise of happiness, behold birth, a wager for the future, the chance to constantly reproduce that which is no more.

However, in the modern world, a world born in the 18th century from a challenge to superstition and religious obscurantism, we know that, in order to prevent the more powerful religions from enslaving human beings, it is necessary to separate the spiritual power to which they lay claim from worldly power which can only rest on the principles of legality, freedom and equality and not on obedience to any system of thought which may have arisen from this or that understanding of the relationship between humanity and its gods, or God.

Since no human society can exist without religion, its best guarantee is the separation of the worldly from the spiritual, of private life from public life, of faith from the exercise of our freedoms. Hence the following paradox: a rule of law, which maintains a neutrality towards any one religion, but tolerates them all, and prevents one from persecuting the other, is the best guarantee of religious freedom, including that of militant atheism, which I consider to be another form of religion.

The danger lies of course, in making science into a religion: scientism or biocracy, which implies the perversion of science. It consists in governing human beings, not by the law or through politics, but through science devolved into technique. This is the form of abuse that has produced Auschwitz; even if today there is no risk of Auschwitz happening again, other forms of biocracy exist and can accommodate themselves very well to all kinds of religious fundamentalism. Remember the famous phrase of Robespierre putting an end to post-Revolutionary attempts to eliminate Christianity:

> He who wishes to prevent the Mass taking place is a greater fanatic than the one who officiates at it. There are men who want to go further, who, under the pretext of destroying superstition want to turn atheism into a kind of religion [...] If God did not exist, we would have to invent him. (Robespierre 1793, Discours à la Convention, 21 November 1793)

I will gladly invoke at this point Elisabeth de Fontenay, who, during a remarkable lecture for children on religion in 2005, said that, even though she herself was 'godless', she liked religions for their 'splendours'.

She added two things: she thought that what enabled her to say this is the fact that the ancestors of her father and her mother (one a Christian, the other a Jew) belonged to two different religions, the one (Christianity) derived from the other, and the fact that this same Christianity had persecuted the other (Judaism) for centuries. I warm to this idea of becoming a materialist through the inheritance of a conflicted genealogy.

She also noted that the philosophers of the Enlightenment never succeeded in converting human beings to the universal cult of Reason and that maybe this was a lucky break; otherwise the world would have become boring, monotonous, without diversity (de Fontenay 2005).

I would add that for my part, even though I remain attached to the universalism of the Enlightenment, and of the dark Enlightenment that Freud and Adorno inherited from Spinoza, Nietzsche and Darwin, I do agree. For as we notice today, for example, during the UN-sponsored Durban conference, Enlightenment reason is, alas, rejected by a majority of the people on Earth. For it is in its name, or, rather, by a perversion of what it stands for, that the West has done its worst: colonialism and later this anonymous imperialism of globalized capitalism. Purely speculative, and hardly 'liberal', it is a new order of the 'golden calf' (Debray 2008), founded on crazy money. The negation of art, it underpins restrictive religious and popular regimes and acts as a means of social normativity. It is a detestable model in that it exploits nations by fostering a belief that economic liberalism will give them access to the highest level of freedom.

Consequently, we are witnessing today a concerted challenging of the Enlightenment *in itself* by formerly colonized and exploited nations. This same impulse informs the lack of civility of the youth of the *banlieue*, who are rebelling against everything. This concerted challenge or revolt is not something that I partake in, of course, but I know that it is impossible to counter by arguments founded on the nostalgia for the past ('it was better in those days') nor by police repression.

I would now like to turn to the ways in which Freudianism may in effect be the inheritor, as indeed I am, of these three cultures, of Ancient Greece, of the Enlightenment and of Judeo-Christianity.

Having founded psychoanalysis, not on a neurological model but on a reading of Darwin, of Sophocles's *Oedipus Rex* and Shakespeare's *Hamlet*, in other words on evolution, on the Greek conception of destiny and on the guilty consciousness proper to Christianity, at the end of his life, a refugee from Nazism, Freud decided to add to this a reflection on Jewishness.

In his last book, published in 1939, *Moses and Monotheism*, Freud reads Judaism as a highly spiritualized religion, similar to the great philosophical thought of the Ancient Greeks. This is a form of monotheism capable of simultaneously renouncing the polytheism of animism and paganism in favour of a unique and invisible God. It is a monotheism that sees itself as carrier of the law and of the word.

Moses becomes the legislator of this monotheism but his people could not accept the weight of this newly acquired spirituality. They killed their prophet and repressed the murderous act. This repression was then transmitted from one generation to the next, whilst monotheism itself was instituted within and through Judaism, dependent on the principle of election, as the divine religion of the primal father.

In Christianity which follows upon Judaism, the murder of the father is expiated by the execution of the son and by the abandonment of circumcision, the visible sign of election.

According to Freud, by giving up circumcision and election, Christianity becomes a universal religion, in other words, it becomes popular, a religion of the masses, and so transforms Judaism into a fossilized knowledge. However, relative to Judaism, the new religion of the son constitutes both an intellectual and a cultural regression. Freud therefore simultaneously valorizes and devalues Judaism. Whilst in his eyes Christianity is progressive due to its universal appeal and the lifting of repression that it leads to, Judaism remains more elitist and carries a greater degree of spirituality.

However, within the scheme of monotheism, Judeo-Christianity constitutes a whole, and it is for this reason that it has become, according to Freud, the target of modern anti-Semitism and National Socialism. Freud writes:

> All those people who excel today in their hatred of the Jews became Christian only in late historic times, often driven to it by bloody coercion. It might be said that they are all 'misbaptised'... They have not got over a grudge against the new religion ... but they have displaced the grudge onto the source from which Christianity has reached them ... Their hatred of Jews is at bottom a hatred of Christians, and we need not be surprised that in the German-National-Socialist revolution this intimate relation between the two monotheist religions finds such a clear expression in the hostile treatment of both of them. (Freud 1939, pp. 91–2)

Between universalized Christianity and 'fossilized' Judaism, there only remains Jewishness, in other words, this specific identity of godless Jews, and only one path, that of eternity, solitude, rootlessness. So Freud clearly separates the sense of belonging to a religion from the sense of belonging (Jewishness) that makes a Jew still feel Jewish, despite having ceased to be religious.

According to Freud, this feeling constitutes a kind of unconscious inheritance transmitted through all eternity as a sign of a renewed sense of belonging. One could say that psychoanalysis constitutes a continuation of this Jewishness, this godless Judaism, and that is probably the reason why it was considered to be a 'Jewish science' by the Nazis. The extermination of psychoanalysis, the means of giving voice to a rootless solitude, had to be planned, at the very same time when various means of exterminating the Jewish 'race' were being considered.

Freud thought that this identity based on belonging, as represented by Jewishness, could be transmitted without any reference to national or ethnic ways of being rooted. Thus he refuses the notion of the promised land as a kind of messianic accomplishment for the subject, in order to place it within the subject itself. Without any faith in Judaism, Freud was not a Zionist but remained faithful to his Jewishness. He did understand the aspirations of the Jewish people for a land but did not wish it to be in Palestine, fearing a perpetual war between Jews and Arabs. Moreover, he did not believe that a territory elsewhere could ever be a solution to anti-Semitism. This was quite a paradoxical position to take, one that has sometimes been taken as supporting the eventual creation of a Jewish state, and at times as rejecting it.

In fact, Freud refused the idea of a promised land and preferred the Jews of the diaspora to the 'territorial' Jews. Freud's promised land lies in the way in which the unconscious is assigned to the subject, in other words in the decentring of consciousness (Roudinesco 2004).

This leads us to conclude that the Freudian subject is simultaneously inhabited by the presence of gods and of God and by the death of God, by a guilty conscience and by a destiny that escapes him. Such a subject is marked by the internalization of exile, and by the search for a genealogy that must be permanently reconstructed so that its history is not effaced. Such is the 'Jewishness' of the Freudian subject.

I must say that, for all these reasons, I feel close to Freud's positions which, without a doubt, resonate with a personal history.

To conclude, I would say that if I have been able to recognize myself in the triple inheritance of Ancient Greece, the Enlightenment and in Judeo-Christianity, it is probably thanks to psychoanalysis.

But I would also have to add that despite the affinities that I feel with Catholicism, which for me has represented a religion of desire, of art and of transgression, I disapprove of most of the decisions taken by the Roman Catholic Church nowadays, concerning abortion, assisted reproduction, the family and homosexuality. All the more so due to the heritage transmitted to me by the man who taught me to be a historian, Father Michel de Certeau, a Jesuit, a homosexual, a Freudian, Michel Foucault's friend, a man who cared for the poor, the excluded, the marginalized and the oppressed. Despite everything, he had kept his faith but was never challenged about his lifestyle by the 'Company of Jesus' – something they must be commended for.

Contemporary Roman Catholicism is not fundamentalist in a manner comparable to Islamism and other religious fundamentalisms, and that is perhaps why it is undergoing such a terrible crisis of vocation. In this, it is in a similar situation to the psychoanalytic community which, given its overly conservative attitudes, also seems to have abandoned Freud's message and finds itself at risk of no longer being able to fight its true enemies who are also those of the enemies of religion: barbarous adepts of science in thrall to militant atheism.

One final word: Freud was wrong in conflating faith and belief to the point of turning religion into a neurotic system, whilst examining the genesis of the religious fact. He never did propose any simple psychological explanation of religion. It is Jacques Lacan, and one can understand why, that the psychoanalytic movement can thank for having been able to abandon a certain kind of vulgar materialism which had led psychoanalysts towards an overly narrow positivist outlook (Roudinesco 1997). Even if one maintains, as I do, that men have created gods in their own image, this does not prevent one from coming face to face with the following question: the intrinsic linking of the human and the divine in a relation of reciprocity. This is perhaps why there were so many Jesuits in Lacan's first circle.

For non-reductionist materialists, the ones who believe in doubt and in reason and not in the certitude of the quantifiable, the divine is part of a myth that presupposes not only belief but also faith. What is implied here, in other words, is something mystical, which Freud did not understand, and which is of the order of a linguistic initiatory experience, whereby the subject accedes to a direct, even logical knowledge of the divine thing, to a revelation that is not madness or illusion, and in which he sees a gift of God that transcends simple belief as much as it transcends institutionalized religion.

For those who participate in such a direct knowledge of God and who therefore are not merely believers, subject to a tradition, to a cult and to an adherence to a Church, with all the attendant risk of going off track in the direction of obscurantism, the divine cannot depend on myth but on a kind of revelation which simultaneously transcends religion and institutes it. This is a gift which comes neither from projection nor from the identification of the subject with a logical God, but from God himself who invites the subject to take a logical wager, the one taken by Saint Anselm or Pascal.

It appears of course that no consensus, no act of conciliation (Cloesens 2008, p. 14), can bring together the two points of view: that of materialist reason, founded on doubt without certitude, and that of faith, founded on logic without obscurantism.

However, what I have wanted to show here is that only the fight against barbarism can reconcile one to the other, 'the one who believes in heaven and the one who does not', as Louis Aragon (2007), the communist poet, put it, at the height of anti-Nazi resistance.

References

Aragon, L. (2007) La rose et le réséda (1941). In: *Poèmes de la Résistance, Oeuvres poétiques complètes*. Paris: Gallimard.

de Certeau, M. (1982) *La Fable mystique*. Paris: Gallimard.

Cloesens, L. (2008) *Le Monde des religions*, March–April.

Debray, R. (2008) *Un Candide en terre sainte*. Paris: Gallimard.

De Fontenay, E. (2005) *Les mille et une fêtes. Petite conférence sur les religions*. Paris: Fayard.

Freud, S. (1939) *Moses and Monotheism. SE* 23, pp. 1–139. London: Hogarth, 1964.

Robespierre, M. (1793) Discours au Club des Jacobins, 21 novembre 1793. *Le Moniteur*, t. 18, p. 508. Paris: Plon, 1860.

Roudinesco, E. (1997) *Jacques Lacan: Outline of a Life, History of a System of Thought*. New York, NY: Columbia University Press.

Roudinesco, E. (2004) A propos d'une lettre inédite de Freud sur le sionisme et la question des lieux saints. *Cliniques méditerranéennes* 70: 6–17.

Roudinesco, E. (2008) *Philosophers in a Turbulent Time*. New York, NY: Columbia University Press.

Scholem, G. (1973) *Les Grands courants de la mystique juive*. Paris: Payot.

ABSTRACT

This paper recounts the author's personal historical relationship with two mono-
theistic religions, Christianity and Judaism. Freud's own understanding of Judaism
as expressed in texts such as *Moses and Monotheism* is discussed, in relation
to the universal aspirations of psychoanalysis. The particular materialism of
Enlightenment philosophy is affirmed, whilst an allowance is made for a certain
kind of mysticism contra the instrumentalization of human beings so prevalent in
contemporary, globalized society.

Key words: Enlightenment, Christianity, Freud, Judaism, Jewishness

DOI: 10.3366/E1460823509000440

FASCISM AND FUNDAMENTALISM:
RESPONSE TO ELISABETH ROUDINESCO

Jacqueline Rose, London, UK

First to say what a privilege I consider it to be to have the opportunity to respond to Elisabeth Roudinesco, whose engagement with psychoanalysis as practitioner, as thinker and as chronicler has been so exemplary and whose interest in the potential link between psychoanalysis and politics goes back many years. I am the proud owner of what I think is perhaps her first, or certainly one of her first, books: *Un discours au réel* of 1973 – almost the same time as Juliet Mitchell's (1974) *Psychoanalysis and Feminism* – and which I remember reading with a real sense of relief because of the energy with which it argued for a dialogue between our understanding of our most contested public, and most passionately guarded private worlds. Central to that book was a thesis in Elisabeth Roudinesco's thinking that I believe has not gone away. That the unconscious, by making a breach in the subject's relation to her historical and social reality, is the place where the false promises and idealizations, the disabling mock unity of an unjust world, are most decisively, repeatedly and painfully undone. From the beginning then, I would suggest, psychoanalysis has been a counter-hegemonic discourse for Roudinesco. 'The place of politics in psychoanalytic practice', she wrote then, 'has no other meaning than that of marking the place of a truth of the unconscious, of a "cut" in the subject's relation to the real' (Roudinesco 1973, p. 17). The politics of that book lay as much in its address to the official psychoanalytic community in danger, as you saw it – indeed then as now – of taming or re-repressing that most disruptive insight of Freud's, as to the world of Marxism–Leninism which at its best only ever allowed a glimpse of it, as well as to the so-called radical Freudians whose naïve, absolutist dream of a liberated psychic and social utopia risked wiping out

JACQUELINE ROSE is Professor of English at Queen Mary University of London. Her publications include: editor (with Juliet Mitchell) and translator, *Feminine Sexuality: Jacques Lacan and the école freudienne* (Macmillan & Pantheon-Norton, 1982), and, more recently, *On Not Being Able to Sleep: Psychoanalysis and the Modern World* (Chatto & Princeton University Press, 2003), *The Question of Zion* (Princeton University Press, 2005) and *The Last Resistance* (Verso, 2007). Address for correspondence: School of English, Queen Mary University of London, Mile End Road, London E1 4NS. [j.rose@qmul.ac.uk]

Psychoanalysis and History 11(2), 2009

the unconscious altogether. Our social reality has of course dramatically changed since then as well as the discourses to which many of us turn in the search for emancipatory potential. But if we are here, it is presumably because in some way psychoanalysis, if only as a question, has somehow remained.

If I think this is relevant to our topic, it is because there is perhaps an unspoken assumption, perhaps something more like a hope or wish to believe, in the radical potential of psychoanalysis, a conviction, shaky but endurable, that psychoanalysis is or can be the enemy, almost by definition, of Fascism and fundamentalism, although we know historically in the first case this not to be true. In fact the title of this conference, 'Psychoanalysis, Fascism and Fundamentalism', is ambiguous, deliberately I assume, by simply listing psychoanalysis as one of three, stringing them along as it were. Such neutrality in itself, I think, took some courage. Nonetheless I think there is also an implied asymmetry in this title which puts psychoanalysis at the head of the triad as if to ward off these two historical monstrosities of the last and present century, which then become – wrongly I would say – twinned or guilty by association. If I am right about that wish, then I would say that the paper by Elisabeth Roudinesco gives to that wish one of its strongest, and most personally felt, articulations. It is a wish I should say that I share. How far we can believe in it is then the question.

First and foremost, of course, your paper is an intensely personal statement of your relationship to Christianity and Judaism as identity and faith. For, while you refuse the latter in both cases, nonetheless you extract from each something of the order of an ethos: the logos of the book from Jewishness, the sensuality of Catholic doctrine. While such sensuality may transgress Catholic stricture, it also flows from the very opulence of Catholic ritual, as well as from prohibitions whose main aim seems to be to invite, indeed welcome, their repeated violation. From both of these religions you take spirit rather than faith. You are willing to be the child neither of Judaism's righteous nor of Christianity's loving God. As you add to these two the heroism of Greek culture, we watch an identity, one which finally lights on the principles of intellect, desire and freedom, sketching itself out consciously and unconsciously in your mind. It would be tempting to say that this makes you the pure product of Western culture: Judeo-Christian and classical Greek, except that this in-mixing of identities leaves not one of them pure or intact. Let's say then that you have described yourself as a promiscuous daughter of the West.

You have therefore located and dislocated yourself at the same time. Perhaps this is why, as I see it, that apparent mixing of identities, or rather forms of allegiance, is also partially deceptive, and why one of these allegiances – simply in the flow of the paper as it unfolds – seems to me to win out, although that might be too strong a term. And that is of course

Jewishness – French *'judéité'* – a way of being Jewish without Judaic faith. It is an identity rooted in memory, and since the memory of the Jewish people is above all to be unrooted, exilic – crucially, although you mention Zionism, you do not mention Israel – then this means that the dislocation proper to these partial, fractured identities comes to reside in, is epitomized above all by, Jewishness itself. As you end your reading of Freud's *Moses and Monotheism*, Jewishness becomes the one path of 'eternity, solitude, rootlessness'. If I read you correctly, your very ability to see yourself as the child of such multiple forms of belonging then becomes Freud's legacy and gift as a non-Jewish Jew to you.

As I had the great pleasure of looking back through your work in preparation for this response, it seemed to me that this question of psychoanalysis's Jewishness is something of a thread, one that works its way as much through your historical as your theoretical engagement with Freud. So your history of psychoanalysis in France – the magisterial two-volume *La bataille de cent ans* – makes Dreyfus central to the early stirrings of psychoanalysis in France (Roudinesco 1982, 1986). From its inception, French psychoanalysis found itself up against anti-Semitism, masquerading as anti-Germanic chauvinism. Freud and his science were seen to represent those debauched and degenerate, alien, forms of Jewishness from which the assimilated Jews of France – precisely known as 'Israelites' rather than 'Jews' – had spent the past half a century and more so carefully trying to distinguish themselves. This is from Volume 1 of your history which appallingly has not been translated into English, history ceding to celebrity, since Volume 2 was translated as *Jacques Lacan and Company* – not your title – as if anything about Lacan can be understood independently of this history. I quote:

> At the moment Freudianism was being introduced in France, the Israelite had become the polished, elegant, version of the Jew, an assimilated citizen above all 'restricted in his desires'. Someone capable of dominating his instincts and repressing his pernicious libido, that same libido which stirred the thoughts of his strange Germanic, Viennese, Hungarian fellow creatures. Thus crudely could the so-called 'pansexualism' of Freud be denounced under the triple banner of germanophobia, unconscious judeophobia and cartesianism. In other words, anti-pansexualism, pitting itself against the Freudian doctrine of sexuality, is always the expression, whether overt or attenuated, of a race psychology which will not speak its name. (Roudinesco 1982, p. 191)

From the beginning therefore, Freud in France was – and I think the argument was as persuasive as it is important – the target of barely disguised racism. The reference to Cartesianism is also crucial, since it is Freud's assault on the idea of a self-possessed ego that is no less the crux of the matter. If the argument was local to France, it is also of far more general import and brings us to Fascism. For you, the Nazi attempt to 'exterminate' psychoanalysis – and I note in your paper that is the word you use – can then be seen as the logical outcome, or final embodiment, of a doctrine of racial purity, grounded in a refusal of body and unconscious, for which Freudian thinking could only be the utmost threat and aberration. As you point out in your wonderful dialogue with Jacques Derrida, 'Eulogy for Psychoanalysis', Hitler went for Freudian psychoanalysis like no other form of psychoanalysis even if, as in the case of Adler, they were also Jewish. You cite Thomas Mann at the time of the *Anschluss*:

> How this man [Hitler] must hate psychoanalysis! Secretly I suspect that the fury with which he marched on a certain capital was basically to do with the old analyst installed there, his true and essential enemy, the philosopher who unmasked neurosis, the great disillusionist. (Roudinesco & Derrida 2001, p. 307)

So Freud's Jewishness is central, but it is Jewishness allied to the theory of the unconscious, as a radical demystification of purity which is the worst offender. The theory of the unconscious and Jewishness together attest to a profound rootlessness, the human's subject's in-depth estrangement from herself. Psychoanalysis then becomes, as Josef Hayim Yerushalmi describes it in his own book on Moses, a metamorphosis of Judaism 'divested of its illusory religious forms' (Yerushalmi 1993, p. 99). 'Is there not', you say in 'Eulogy for Psychoanalysis', 'something in the Freudian concept of the unconscious which touches on an invisible universal of which judeity would be the mirror image?' (Roudinesco & Derrida 2001, pp. 307–8).

I think this is one of the strongest arguments for the challenge that psychoanalysis poses to Fascism. There is also a kind of poetic justice in the fact that this challenge draws its character from the history of the very people the Nazis wanted to exterminate. You also locate that challenge more precisely still in the critique of tyranny that can be drawn from Freud's emphasis on the wounded, oedipal father. An undone, humiliated father, prone to a symbolic law whose burden he also bears, takes the place of the archaic, authoritarian sovereignty of the tyrant. Or, to put it more simply, in your reading of psychoanalysis, the father's claim to embody the law is hollow and his tyranny – hence all tyranny – undone. This has also been a constant strand in your thinking and indeed life as a psychoanalyst, notably in relation to the complex embodiment and undoing of paternity in the figure of Lacan. I am thinking here of the open letter you wrote to him in 1977 on the question of his training procedure *la passe* which you described as an 'instrument of a madness for power' (Roudinesco 1986, p. 638).

If that were all, it would already be quite a lot. But you do not stop there. And the other move of your paper is, I think, even more remarkable and perhaps unexpected while also leading us to the question of fundamentalism that is our other theme. I note, and I am sure I am not alone in noting, that Islam as the third of the great faiths is not mentioned by you. You make no false claims of affinity or understanding. In his dialogue with you, Derrida argues that Islam has remained basically inaccessible to psychoanalysis. But I do not think you would want to place this failure, if that is what it is, at the door of Islam, or perhaps I like to think you wouldn't, although I may well be wrong on this. You have after all been an outspoken critic, not just of psychoanalysis's complicity with authoritarian regimes in Latin America, but also for the way it has blundered, culture-blind, into new worlds such as Eastern Europe and China. You are, we could say, alert to psychoanalysis's own colonizing impulses.

But if I would prefer not to see any implied critique of Islam here, it is because there is another strand in this paper, which, I think, could apply to each of the great monotheisms, which draws on a type of spirituality of which fundamentalism would be the travesty. I note that on the question of religion – specifically by confusing belief and faith – you say that Freud was 'wrong'. I have personally always thought that *The Future of an Illusion* was his least Freudian text and was delighted to read in your history of psychoanalysis of the discussion between Freud and René Laforgue in which, as Laforgue recorded it in his diary, Freud describes it as his worst book (Roudinesco 1982, p. 407). Contra Freud as it were, therefore, you distinguish religion and spirituality. And to this form of spirituality, which at moments you term mystic, you assign a type of 'invisible universal' value, exactly as you did to Jewishness and the unconscious. Militant atheism and scientific barbarism, or barbaric scientism, are its modern enemies because they so ruthlessly suppress the interiority to which spiritual experience attests. In this, I would say you align yourself implicitly with those who criticize fundamentalism in the name of true religion, arguing that fundamentalism is a violently distorted manifestation of the very spirituality it claims to represent. I am thinking here of someone like Karen Armstrong (2000) whose argument has consistently been that West must take its share of responsibility for fundamentalism, not just because it was a US export, but because the aggressive secularity with which it has pursued its agendas has suppressed the vestiges of true spiritual life.

The key link for you here is, I believe, Michel de Certeau, who was of course your teacher and inspiration. So you sent me back to his writings on mysticism, *La fable mystique* (de Certeau 1982) and his translated essay 'Mystic speech' (de Certeau 1986) which distils so much of his thought. For de Certeau, the link between mysticism and psychoanalysis was profound. Mysticism is a form of speech that has, I quote, 'the power to induce departure'; it radically dissociates itself from the world in the name of interiority, it subjects its practitioner, although that is not the right word, to a form of radical rootlessness (de Certeau 1986, p. 83). The mystic is

Wandersmann, the Wanderer. Mystical experience thus becomes – and you will have all seen where this is leading – almost, almost, another word for the unconscious:

> Mystical is the one who cannot stop walking and who, certain of what he lacks, knows of each place and each object, that that is *not it*, that she or he cannot reside *here*, cannot be content with *that*. Desire creates an excess that goes beyond, overtakes and loses all place. It leads you beyond, somewhere else. It lives nowhere. (de Certeau 1982, p. 411)

Is it right to say therefore that, in relation to fundamentalism, mystical experience takes up the place that psychoanalysis and Jewishness occupied in the earlier encounter with Fascism? And since I read both mysticism and Jewishness in this line of thought as other words for the unconscious, am I right in thinking that for you the unconscious returns as the supreme counter to the perils of fundamentalism? In which case we have surely come full circle.

I started by saying that I thought the title of this Conference risks an elision between Fascism and fundamentalism. I myself would want to make a crucial distinction between Fascism as the tyrannical embodiment, if not deification, of the reason of state; and fundamentalism which, as you do also point out, is mostly aligned with powerlessness or, to use Caroline Rooney's evocative phrase, with 'chronic disappointment', even if its fantasy is to rule the world. I would want, that is, to distinguish between actualization and longing. In our rush to condemn fundamentalism we also need to remind ourselves constantly of the extent to which it is often our creation, born of the Western legacy to which your paper acknowledges its own deep personal affinity, which might be read – although in fact I think this is my projection – as a call for accountability in itself. Nonetheless if I have read you rightly, psychoanalysis remains for you today a discourse – or should I say – *the* discourse '*au réel*'. That is to say, it is where we should continue to look for a way of thought that most radically challenges systems of belief that today seem once again to have the power to place the whole world in peril.

References

Armstrong, K. (2000) *The Battle for God: Fundamentalism in Judaism, Christianity and Islam*. London: Harper Collins.
de Certeau, M. (1982) *La fable mystique*, vol. 1, *XVIe–XVIIe siècle*. Paris: Gallimard.
de Certeau, M. (1986) Mystic speech. In: *Heterologies – Discourse on the Other*, pp. 80–100, trans. B. Massumi. Minneapolis, MN: University of Minnesota Press; Manchester: Manchester University Press, 1996.
Mitchell, J. (1974) *Psychoanalysis and Feminism*. London: Allen Lane.
Roudinesco, E. (1973) *Un discours au réel: Théorie de l'inconscient et politique de la psychanalyse*. Paris: Mame.

Roudinesco, E. (1982) *La bataille de cent ans: Histoire de la psychanalyse en France*, vol. 1, *1885–1939*. Paris: Seuil.

Roudinesco, E. (1986) *La bataille de cent ans: Histoire de la psychanalyse en France*, vol. 2, *1925–1985*. Paris: Seuil. [(1990) *Jacques Lacan & Co.*, trans. J. Mehlman. London: Free Association Books.]

Roudinesco, E. & Derrida, J. (2001) De quoi demain ... Dialogue. In: *Eloge de la psychanalyse*, pp. 171–7. Paris: Fayard/Galilée.

Yerushalmi, Y.H. (1993) *Freud's Moses: Judaism Terminable and Interminable*. New Haven, CT, London: Yale University Press.

ABSTRACT

This paper, a response to Elisabeth Roudinesco's lecture in this collection, argues that her work has been sustained from the outset by a psychoanalytic critique of political identifications via the concept of the unconscious, that the concept of Judeity or Jewishness has been central to that critique, and that it finds its most recent manifestation in a defence of mystical experience against a new secular theology.

Key words: psychoanalysis, Fascism, Nazism, fundamentalism, Jewishness, mysticism

DOI: 10.3366/E1460823509000452

AFTERWORD: PSYCHOANALYSIS, FASCISM, FUNDAMENTALISM AND ATHEISM

John Forrester, Cambridge, UK

The conference on 'Psychoanalysis, Fascism and Fundamentalism' which produced the papers which this Journal is pleased to publish was an intense, stimulating and memorable event. As one hopes of such a conference, it produced as many questions as it answered. Yet none of the speakers picked out one odd feature of linking the three nouns together to make a title and a theme. Psychoanalysis is a science and a therapeutic practice, Fascism is a political ideology and a political practice and fundamentalism is, following the *OED*, a movement advocating strict adherence to certain tenets held to be fundamental (i.e. non-negotiable or not open to question) to a religious faith. So three movements: one quasi-scientific, one political, one religious. Why bring these three different worlds together?

Finding an answer to this question may be helped by noting a further oddity – a coincidence that may be more than that. Fascism was born in Italy in the wake of the First World War; although psychoanalysis was formed as a theory and a programme in the first two decades of the 20th century, it only became a movement with a major cultural resonance, whose ripples from a certain moment onwards extended very widely and with no coordinated control through the arts and sciences, in the same historical moment – in the wake of the First World War. Strikingly, fundamentalism as a term and a movement also dates from the same moment; the *OED* gives a first usage in English-American in 1923 (*Daily Mail*, 24 May 1923, p. 8: 'Mr. William Jennings Bryan has been exerting the full force of his great eloquence in a campaign on behalf of what is termed "Fundamentalism"'), with a usefully indicative usage in 1925 from the journal *Relig. Yesterday & To-morrow*: 'There has been in America some surprise at the sudden rise of Fundamentalism in the last five years.' The third *OED* reference, from *The Observer* in 1927, even points – inadvertently? is this *another* coincidence? – to a link between fundamentalism and Fascism: 'Fundamentalism and the

---

JOHN FORRESTER is Professor of History and Philosophy of the Sciences at the University of Cambridge and Editor of *Psychoanalysis and History*. Address for correspondence: [jpf11@cam.ac.uk]

Psychoanalysis and History 11(2), 2009

Ku Klux Klan are signs of alarm on behalf of the older ideals'. As I read these entries, I sense the Editors of the *OED* are trying to tell us something.

Reflecting on this chronological simultaneity of origin for Fascism, fundamentalism and psychoanalysis might strengthen our conviction that these movements are each responses to, or children of, the economic and cultural modernity that had transformed politics, religion and science. It is not controversial to assume that psychoanalysis is a form of modernism – allied to Darwinism, to positivism, to the rise of sexology – and embodies one of the most challenging of the new developments of modernism in the early 20th century: the attempt to give an account of the intimate and moral life of the individual in scientific, rather than religious, terms. Psychoanalysis certainly appeared to the opposing forces of Fascism and Nazism on the one hand, and conservative religious movements on the other, as an unclean and profane attack on the Fascist virtues and the values of purified Christianity. Attacks on psychoanalysis by the Vatican or conservative psychiatrists in the name of the moral health of the medical profession were part of the politics of the psychoanalytic movement from the 1910s on. But such disputes were conducted for the most part roughly within the intact codes of behaviour – sometimes contested or flouted, with singular lapses – of freedom and respect for institutional, professional and personal autonomy set within 'civil society'. What we recognize as the Fascist innovation was the direct subordination of such institutions in civil society to the legislative authority of the State; and psychoanalysis was particularly singled out as a target for destruction in the name of the many social and cultural transformations induced by the rise of the Fascist State.

Until the Iranian revolution, 'fundamentalism' simply named the conservative strands of American Protestantism. In other words, the term 'fundamentalism' was revived to describe a new political formation – the 'Islamic revolution' linked with State power. Is there historical coherence or plausibility, or even new understanding, to be got from comparing the history of Fascism in the mid-20th century with the development of forms of Islam – the 'Islams' Massad reminds us of in this volume – allied with the State at the end of the 20th century? By using the American term 'fundamentalism' in conjunction with the European term 'Fascism', an implicit question is posed: can religion be the foundation of a regime analogous to Fascism?

Fascism shared with religious communities (whether allied with the State, distanced from it, or even in opposition to it) a preoccupation with the reordering of the everyday life of citizens, in particular, because of its concern for the population of the nation and for reproductive regimes, for their sexual and moral lives. So it is natural – in the sense of 'true to its very nature' – for religion to share with Fascism a similar preoccupation and temptation to develop a politics governing the life of the family, the relations between the sexes and the regime of the forbidden and permitted in sexual life. (Of course – foreshadowing a later argument – it would also be tempting to see Fascism as historically responding to a failure of religion to fulfil this function satisfactorily in the new modernist era of the interwar years and as deriving some of its cultural purchase from this supplanting of and borrowing from these traditional functions of religion.)

It is in this arena of the private and the sexual life that psychoanalysis was and still is so obviously implicated. Reflections such as Freud's: 'It is one of the obvious social injustices that the standard of civilization should demand from everyone the same conduct of sexual life' (Freud 1908, p. 192) might have some purchase in a liberal democracy but are anathema to any regime which develops as part of its core policies State regulations and positive injunctions concerning sexual and reproductive life. Or so it would seem. Psychoanalysis was by no means the only new science or discipline making claims for authoritative knowledge and efficacious practices in the domain of sexuality, reproduction and the regulation of behaviour. Eugenics was the most notorious but by no means the only example: this was also the era of the development of reproductive physiology and endocrinology alongside criminology and psychiatry. Eugenics became the epitome of the tainted science, not least because of the part it played in racial planning within the Nazi state; from then on, one crucial element of the spectre of Fascism that haunted the late-20th century was the regulation of moral, sexual and reproductive life at the expense of the individual, through the prohibition of certain sexual practices, through the governing of the population by means of racial laws and through the control of women's bodies.

Through a ruse of reason, within modern biopolitics the functions intended to be performed by eugenics have been successfully revived in a market-driven, individualized form, in the endocrinological developments that led to the introduction of hormonal control (the contraceptive pill) and in the technologies of assisted reproduction to which advances in reproductive physiology gave rise. The regulation and promotion of these new forms of eugenics do not conform straightforwardly to the division between liberal and authoritarian regimes, let alone theocratic regimes, that studies preoccupied with Fascism and its struggle with liberal democracy might predict. The Iranian state has promoted the development of sophisticated facilities for assisted reproduction while maintaining strict conditions about the interaction between the sexes, whether professionals or parents, in these procedures; in contrast, France and Germany have reacted with State-sanctioned moral repugnance to some of these technologies – hence the illegality of surrogate motherhood in both these jurisdictions.

The historic position of psychoanalysis as being in the vanguard of modernist reform – through opposition to laws governing sexual behaviour, through criticism of parental authoritarianism and of the religious grounding of morals – together with its unsavoury allies in bohemian and free-thinking artistic circles found itself undercut by the ever-increasing tendency to produce conventional and conformist professional leaders of its ever more staid institutions. The increasingly disapproving, even sniffy, attitude of psychoanalysts to transformations in sexual mores, to sexual politics crossed with identity politics, to family formats that deviate from the oedipal, even to laws that permitted one to marry someone of one's own 'gender' and to choose one's own gender,[1] has been palpable for several decades. If the early years of psychoanalysis could be accused of producing enthusiasts and prophets, its maturity was more amply endowed with guardians and priests. This pattern matched the perception of its sympathetic critics, who saw its historical destiny as residing in its capacity to perform the function of religion without the theological apparatus of belief and the divine. A secular religion for a scientific age, Gellner diagnosed; yet also a modern science whose practitioners practised literalist interpretation of their sacred texts (Freud, Lacan) and were bound to accept without discussion its 'fundamentals' – its 'shibboleths' and 'cornerstones'. And, while its ethos was avowedly cosmopolitan, secular and entirely imbued with the values of civil society crossed with the newly professionalizing sciences, it never came to an adequate explanation or self-understanding of why its origins and its later development were so closely allied with the destiny of the secular Jews of Europe and America.

While its most stringent critics were never wholly convincing in their claim that the cultic structure of psychoanalysis reduced it to the status of another new sect, akin perhaps to Christian Science, its defenders could point to the radical departure in its practical project of instructing how to live without belief (Rieff 1979, p. 305). The aim of psychoanalysis is to strip away the illusions, principally those of religion, but also those of politics, insofar as they may originate in perpetual infantile helplessness, producing the same servile obedience and the same vain hope for the care of authority. The formula 'living without belief' is certainly agnostic in its tenor. There was one side of Freud, the Enlightenment Freud, last or, at least, late in the line of the castigators of priests and Grand Inquisitors, champion of science, scourge of the pitiful illusions by which humans live, chief amongst which was religion – the Freud who would write *The Future of an Illusion*, perhaps in response to the Scopes Trial which was the most publicized aspect of the ferment that gave rise to American fundamentalism. This is the Freud who is closely in tune with the radical secularists who, in France, enacted

---

1. As in the UK *Gender Recognition Act* 2004: 'A person of either gender who is aged at least 18 may make an application for a gender recognition certificate on the basis of living in the other gender ... Where a full gender recognition certificate is issued to a person, the person's gender becomes for all purposes the acquired gender (so that, if the acquired gender is the male gender, the person's sex becomes that of a man and, if it is the female gender, the person's sex becomes that of a woman).'

the law of 9 December 1905 making explicit the separation of Church and State. This was the most prominent of the series of laws enacted under the Third Republic (including laws banning religious symbols, particularly any crucifix larger than a certain size) restricting the power of the Catholic Church in civil life, in particular in education. (It was these laws restraining religion which would enable the banning of Fascist propaganda in French schools in 1937.) It is the extension of these laws, controversially, to Islamic 'symbols' – the *foulard*, the headscarf – which Davids, in this volume, takes to be a 'a systematic, institutionalized assault' on civil liberties.[2]

However, alongside the enthusiastically secularist Enlightenment Freud, this Freud who saw, like so many others, the exclusion of religion and politics, the exclusion of traditional social ties as the best and most civilized way for egalitarianism to triumph and the Jews and other disadvantaged groups to gain access to civil society, there is what Adam Phillips has called the 'post-Freudian Freud' (Phillips 1995, p. 12) – the ironist of the project of Enlightenment, of self-knowledge, whose quiet voice of reason is pitted against grandiose claims, even those of justice and equality, perhaps even those of psychoanalysis. This, one might hope, with some grounds for its truth, is the voice of the practising analyst – the not-knowing analyst, whose practice exemplifies the analytic virtues, who can 'tolerate ambivalence and uncertainty' (Borossa & Ward, 'Foreword', this volume). This is the practising analyst, like Davids, who, alongside his sense of the scandal of an attack on human rights by the French state, can tolerate the hostile, potentially murderous life-choices of a fledgling terrorist and recast fundamentalism as a valuable cultural resource, 'by providing a vehicle for living out, and hence containing, their inner adolescent conflict'. It is this analytic virtue that then gives rise to a more quietistic, yet ultimately more subversive, ethic – the 'ethic of honesty', the 'little communions of counter-belief' which Philip Rieff described as the psychoanalytic alternative to both politics and religion.

Is living without belief the same as atheism? It might be viewed as the psychoanalytic form of atheism, as opposed to the evangelical form of atheism which has arisen recently, to counter the sporadic surges of religiosity that some Western cultures have inexplicably suffered from in recent years. Most of the inhabitants of Western Europe live without religious conviction and with little or no exercise of the rituals of religious observance. Many of those who attend church, mosque or synagogue may

---

2. It has struck me as curious how contemptuous has been much British and American commentary on the French laws governing dress code in schools; the British in particular were and are rather enthusiastic about the civilizing *and* egalitarian function of school uniform. Certainly when I was at school in the UK a boy who came to school without a tie would be sent home peremptorily; his reasons for not wearing a tie were irrelevant. When it came to school discipline, the exceptionless blindness (even-handedness) was the whole point.

pay little heed to matters of dogma and 'belief'.[3] Many Europeans are now genuinely bewildered by the force of religion in other people's lives, not sure if they should be scared or reassured by the obvious analogies of recent history – the waves of football hooligans, so much a part of recent European history, or the extreme nationalist terrorist groups (IRA, ETA). For these bewildered born-atheists, there is a temptation to treat religion simply as a source of social unrest, precisely because of the passions it arouses in its supporters – akin to the passion for a United Ireland or the passion for Manchester United.

So it is as if psychoanalysis offers two different approaches to such questions, two varieties of atheism even. The first is vigorous sceptical atheism, easily aligned with the new evangelical atheism (Dawkins *et al.*). The second is that methodological atheism intrinsic to the practice of psychoanalysis, but now emerging as a truly radical atheism, attempting to find the sources for the passion expressed in religious belief. An analogy may help. At its inception, psychoanalysis recognized homosexuality as a perversion, an exemplary perversion because of the cultural and historical pervasiveness of the practice, its lack of grounding in any hereditary determination and the graphic manner in which it demonstrated the contingency of sexual object-choice. At the same time, psychoanalysts were vigorous in their opposition to the criminalization of homosexuality. However, distinctive psychoanalytic accounts of the origins of homosexuality became an important part of psychoanalytic theory: in the identification with a beloved mother, in a distinctive set of identifications produced in the resolution of the Oedipus complex. Such explanations became anathema in the era of identity politics initiated in the 1970s. Homosexuals, many might claim, were born not made: that is what it meant to have an identity. The practices of psychoanalysts aimed at transforming homosexuals into heterosexuals came to be regarded as coercive impositions of normative heterosexuality. But, it might plausibly be argued, what is the point of psychoanalysis if it is not the search for the hidden, the unconscious sources of one's favoured desires, one's most compulsive and treasured of desires? That is the job of the psychoanalyst.

By analogy, the search for the sources of one's religious faith must be a part of any psychoanalysis worthy of being called such. (The religious

---

3. They may be like my late friend and colleague Peter Lipton (though usually without his need for consistency and omnipresent humour), who described himself as a 'religious atheist'. A philosopher, he wished to explain how he could arrive at such a position. 'For some religious people, the satisfaction they derive from their religion would evaporate if they ceased to believe in the existence and influence of God. But for others, it is not belief that is doing the work, but rather intense and communal engagement with religious text and with religious practice ... by distinguishing acceptance from belief [this solution] finds a way to achieve consistency of belief without effacing incompatibility of content. On this approach, we preserve content by adjusting our attitude towards it. We have literalism without fundamentalism; inconsistency without irrationality' (Lipton 2009, p. 19).

observances of the Wolf Man's childhood and their transformations would obviously be exemplary of this inevitable and uncontentious therapeutic programme.) Religious faith and practices would have the same standing as a sexual perversion (such as homosexuality). Methodological atheism requires the discarding of norms in the sphere of religion in the same way as the analysis of sexual perversion requires the discarding of moral norms concerning sexual behaviour. One could not expect a psychoanalyst to act otherwise. The evangelical atheist psychoanalyst would be as inappropriate as the seducing homosexual analyst. Every analyst knows that heterosexuality can be as perverse a defensive structure as any other mode of sexual behaviour and s/he certainly doesn't allow the recognition that the human genitals are biologically fitted for what is archly known as heterosexual intercourse to interfere with the appreciation of the architecture of sexual perversion. However, the methodological – the working, everyday – atheist is constitutive of psychoanalysis.

History pulled a surprise on psychoanalysis with the return of religion in the last third of the 20th century – a return that went hand in hand with the de-Europeanization of world politics, the unravelling of Europe's intellectual hegemony and the irreversible burial of colonial and imperial models of politics and social order. The analogy with homosexuality and other sources of the identity politics (special interest politics, single-issue politics) that replaced the grand narratives of Left and Right is again helpful. The sea-change in politics was as significant for the destiny of psychoanalysis as the undoubtedly crucial shifts in the cognate mental and bodily sciences of the period, the new reproductive technologies and the psychopharmacological revolution. Expelled from the order of the sciences, psychoanalysis also appeared out of tune with political transformations, in which the return of religion could re-appear, on the model of identity politics, as fundamentally political in character. In this light, the reticence of psychoanalysis in relation to the rise of Fascism in the mid-20th century could be interpreted as a good omen: that reticence may well have been the properly psychoanalytic posture to adopt.[4] The question that faces psychoanalysis in relation to fundamentalism – whether or not the analogy between Fascism and fundamentalism can be drawn with any plausibility – is: can its methodological atheism be maintained as the appropriate, even efficacious, position to adopt? Or should psychoanalysis realize that its other natural posture – its active scepticism mutating into vigorous egalitarianism and affirmation of the absoluteness of freedom of speech and the ethic of honesty – ought to govern its relations to the new world of religion and politics?

---

4. This judgement as to the reticence of psychoanalysis should be qualified, as Daniel Pick points out in his paper in this volume.

References

Freud, S. (1908) 'Civilized' sexual morality and modern nervous illness. SE 9, pp. 180–204. London: Hogarth.

Lipton, P. (2009) Science and religion: The immersion solution. In: J. Cornwell and M. McGhee (eds), *Philosophers and God: At the frontiers of faith and reason*, pp. 1–20. London: Continuum.

Phillips, A. (1995) *Terrors and Experts*. London, Boston, MA: Faber and Faber.

Rieff, P. (1979) *Freud: The Mind of the Moralist*. 3rd edn. Chicago, IL: Chicago University Press.

DOI: 10.3366/E1460823509000464

INSTRUCTIONS TO AUTHORS

PSYCHOANALYSIS AND HISTORY is a peer-reviewed journal devoted both to the study of the history of psychoanalysis and to the application of psychoanalytic ideas to historiography. The interdisciplinary aim of the journal is to form a bridge between the academic study of history and psychoanalysis.

Articles are published in English, with abstracts in the original language if the article appears in translation. **Manuscripts should be submitted electronically** if at all possible to: **John Forrester** <jpf11@cam.ac.uk> The word-processing program for both Windows and Macs should be Microsoft Word; authors may wish to submit in RTF (Rich Text Format) in order to ensure safe arrival. If it is not practicable to submit electronically, four copies of the manuscript should be submitted to: Prof. John Forrester, Editor, *Psychoanalysis and History*, Dept. of History and Philosophy of Science, University of Cambridge, Free School Lane, Cambridge CB2 3RH, UK. Authors considering submitting work in languages other than English should make a preliminary enquiry of the Editor.

MANUSCRIPTS should be typed double-spaced on one side of the page, with generous margins. The average length of articles should be between 6000 and 8000 words, and a word count should be included. An abstract of no more than 150 words should accompany the article, along with a separate page giving author's affiliation and address for correspondence. The author's name should appear only on the title page.

In-text references should be shown as follows: (Gay 1988) or (Gay 1988, pp. 143–7). All direct quotations should have a page reference, using minimum numbering as in the example given.

The list of references should be supplied in one of the main versions of the Harvard style, as in the following examples:

Sole-authored book: Gay, P. (1988) *Freud: A Life for Our Time*. New York: Norton.
Co-authored book: Laplanche, J. & Pontalis, J.-B. (1973) *The Language of Psycho-Analysis*. London: Hogarth.
Chapter in author's own collection:Winnicott, D.W. (1954) Withdrawal and regression. In D.W. Winnicott, *Through Paediatrics to Psychoanalysis*. New York: Basic Books, 1975, pp. 255–61.
Chapter in edited collection: Stern, D. (1983) Implications of infancy research for psychoanalytic theory and practice. In L. Grinspoon (ed.), *Psychiatry Update*. Washington, DC: American Psychiatric Association.
Journal article: Samson, A. (1998) Science, metaphor and meaning in *The Interpretation of Dreams*. *British Journal of Psychotherapy* 14(3): 327–36.

References should be double-spaced, and placed in alphabetical order at the end of the article after any Notes, Acknowledgements, etc. Provided the author is consistent, minor variants on the Harvard style shown above are acceptable in presentation of the references.

Electronic citations   These should be in the form:
Author's surname, rest of name, date of document, Title of document, <web address>, date accessed. The URL (Uniform Resource Locator) begins with a code for the type of access involved: "http://", "ftp://", "gopher://", etc. If the document is dated internally, use that date for the citation. In addition, supply the date at which it was first accessed, e.g.

Lacan, Jacques (1962) 'Séminaire du 14 mars 1962' *Séminaire IX. L'Identification*, http://gaogoa.free.fr/ID14031962.htm, accessed 17.3.2004

EDINBURGH UNIVERSITY PRESS
22 GEORGE SQUARE
EDINBURGH EH8 9LF
Telephone: 0131 650 4218
Fax: 0131 662 0053
www.eup.ed.ac.uk

PSYCHOANALYSIS AND HISTORY ISSN 1460-8235

EDITOR JOHN FORRESTER

PSYCHOANALYSIS AND HISTORY IS A PEER-REVIEWED JOURNAL
DEVOTED BOTH TO THE STUDY OF THE HISTORY OF
PSYCHOANALYSIS AND THE APPLICATION OF PSYCHOANALYTIC
IDEAS TO HISTORIOGRAPHY, THUS FORMING AN
INTERDISCIPLINARY BRIDGE BETWEEN THE ACADEMIC STUDY OF
HISTORY AND PSYCHOANALYSIS.

VOLUME 12ɪ 2010

WILL INCLUDE

Anaclitic Therapy in North American Psychoanalytic
and Psychiatric Practice in the 1950s–1960s
Mical Raz

PSYCHOANALYSIS AND HISTORY IS PUBLISHED TWICE A YEAR

ANNUAL SUBSCRIPTION (VOLUMES 12ɪ & 12ɪɪ)

		UK	RoW	N. America
Institutions	Print	£73.50	£80.00	$152.00
	Online	£66.00	£66.00	$126.00
	Print and online	£92.00	£100.00	$191.00
	Back issues/single copies	£39.00	£41.00	$78.00
Individuals	Print	£33.50	£36.50	$70.00
	Online	£30.00	£30.00	$58.00
	Print and online	£42.00	£45.50	$87.50
	Back issues/single copies	£18.00	£20.00	$38.00

NAME .... ADDRESS..

....

COUNTRY..POSTCODE......................... PH/6

VISA/MASTERCARD   EXPIRY DATE __ __/__ __

SIGNATURE.......................

| | | | | | | | | | | | | | | |

✉ **EDINBURGH UNIVERSITY PRESS, 22 GEORGE SQUARE,
EDINBURGH EH8 9LF**
Tel: 0131 650 4218, Fax 0131 662 0053 www.eup.ed.ac
Address for MSS: Prof. John Forrester <jpf11@cam.ac.uk>
If electronic submission is not possible, printed MSS should be sent to:
Prof. John Forrester, Dept. of History and Philosophy of Science, University of
Cambridge, Free School Lane, Cambridge CB2 3RH, UK
** Back issues available upon request **

EUP JOURNALS ONLINE
www.eupjournals.com

Edinburgh University Press has been an established publisher of scholarly publications for almost 60 years and is one of the largest university presses in the UK. We publish prestigious, long-established journals and quality, peer-reviewed new journals in a range of subject areas covering the arts, humanities, social sciences and science.

2009 Journals

- African Studies
- Historical Studies
- Islamic & Middle Eastern Studies
- Linguistics
- Literary Studies
- Film, Media and Cultural Studies
- Philosophy and Religion
- Politics and Law
- Science and Medical

Features of EUP Journals Online

- Article Citation Tracking
- Bibliographic Information Downloads
- Table of Contents Alerting Service
- Supplementary Material
- CrossRef Cited-by Linking
- Featured Articles
- News and Announcements
- PDF Plus with Hyperlinking of References

Free Sample Issue

Free sample issues of our journals are available on our website. Simply visit a journal's homepage and click the 'All issues' tab to be directed to the free content.

Table of Contents Alerting Service

Register at **www.eupjournals.com** to receive alerts when new content in your field of interest is uploaded to the site, and to view sample issues and featured articles for free.

Edinburgh University Press

Register to receive Table of Contents Alerts at www.eupjournals.com

EU Authorised Representative:

Easy Access System Europe Mustamäe tee 50, 10621 Tallinn, Estonia

gpsr.requests@easproject.com

Printed and bound by CPI Group (UK) Ltd, Croydon, CR0 4YY

22/04/2026

02095385-0001